# Many Voices

# Many Voices:
# Music and National Identity
# in Aotearoa/New Zealand

Edited by

## Henry Johnson

Many Voices:
Music and National Identity in Aotearoa/New Zealand,
Edited by Henry Johnson

This book first published 2010

Cambridge Scholars Publishing

12 Back Chapman Street, Newcastle upon Tyne, NE6 2XX, UK

British Library Cataloguing in Publication Data
A catalogue record for this book is available from the British Library

ISBN (10): 1-4438-2124-1, ISBN (13): 978-1-4438-2124-7

# CONTENTS

**Part II: Popular Culture**

**Part III: Education and High-Art**

**Epilogue**

# ACKNOWLEDGEMENTS

This book would not have been possible without the generous support of various people and institutions. The conference on which this volume is based was sponsored by the Centre for Research on National Identity and the Department of Music, University of Otago. A number of people have given generous time and effort to help with the conference and the proceedings: Alistair Fox, John Drummond, Dan Bendrups, Ian Chapman, Shelley Brunt, Stephen Steadman, Dorothy Duthie, Mary-Jane Campbell, Alison Crossan, Emily Ross, Keith Duthie, Marian Poole, and Peter Scott. Lastly, Cambridge Scholars Publishing are thanked for their help in publishing this book and their continued support for this project.

# CHAPTER ONE

# INTRODUCTION

# HENRY JOHNSON

The age of the nation-state provides geographic boundaries that countries can call their own. While often contested locally, regionally, and on the international stage, these borders can provide markers of identity that group people on a level of national distinction regardless of any other discerning trait with which people might ordinarily identify. Within such borders, individuals might have a cultural identity that is related to notions of being or becoming,[1] or may live transcultural or transnational lives where ideas of national identity are obfuscated across real and imagined borders. One consequence of the nation-state is that notions of national identity are often challenged and continually changing, affected by both top down and bottom up influences. Some of the changes in national identity are brought about by social and cultural flows, such as through the influence of music. The relationship between music and national identity might be viewed in two separate ways. Firstly, there is music that has the objective of either representing a nation or being representative of a nation. Secondly, there are the musics that exist within a nation that may have distinct sources or influences from outside a nation's political borders.

This collection of short papers is the result of a conference held in 2009 as part of a research project within the Centre for Research on National Identity at the University of Otago, New Zealand. The conference, which was entitled "Many Voices: New Zealand Music and National Identity," was organized by the Department of Music with the aim of contributing to discourse on music and national identity in Aotearoa/New Zealand. The conference attracted a number of scholars from New Zealand's North and South Islands, as well as keynote speaker

---

[1] Stuart Hall, "Cultural identity and Diaspora," in *Identity: Community, Culture, Difference*, ed. Jonathan Rutherford (London: Lawrence & Wishart, 1990), 225.

Tony Mitchell from Australia. As a New Zealander working in Australia, Mitchell was himself an example of a level of geographic dislocation that further points to the complexities of national identity and global flows. That is, as people and culture continue to move within, between, and across national and cultural borders, the defining factor of what actually constitutes a national or even cultural music is increasing blurred.

The reason for linking music with the notion of national identity at this conference had much to do with celebrating and discussing cultural diversity in connection with music. The macro and micro musics[2] discussed in many of the papers help show cultural diversity on the one hand, and, on the other hand link that heterogeneity with the geo-politics that has so often been connected with ethnicity and identity. For instance, when researching any musical style, genre, or piece, the simple question, "What role does this music have in this context?" inherently connects to people, whether in a specific localized setting or linked to the broader context of the nation-state.

Aotearoa/New Zealand has done much in recent decades to maintain its British colonial ties, while simultaneously seeking to find its own national identity. How, one might ask, can the two drives co-exist? Even as I write this introductory section, the *New Zealand Herald* has a front page spread challenging the nation's flag with its embedded Union Jack.[3] The call for a New Zealand republic periodically surfaces;[4] and in a post-European era when New Zealand was left to find new trading and political partners the nation-state quickly moved to find its place in the Asia-Pacific region. Moreover, in the past few years, New Zealand has carefully negotiated various free-trade agreements, its most successful perhaps being with the People's Republic of China in 2008. In this context, it seems only logical to locate diverse musics and complex cultural settings within discourses on national identity. After all, how can music be truly understood if its contexts of production, distribution, and consumption are not considered?

Just as nation-states have musical cannons, so there have been traditional ways of writing about New Zealand music. One of the most surprising aspects of scholarly work on music in Aotearoa/New Zealand is the lack of celebration of the diversity and creativity of the music that can

---

[2] Mark Slobin, *Subcultural Sounds: Micromusics of the West* (Hanover: University Press of New England, 1993).
[3] Derek Cheng, Simon Collins, and Wayne Thompson. "We need a new flag it's time for a change," *New Zealand Herald*, February 4, 2010, http://www.knowledge-basket.co.nz.
[4] See http://www.republic.org.nz.

be found in both established and more recent cultural settings. Many institutions do much to celebrate the creativity of New Zealand musicians, but budget constraints mean that even organizations such as the Centre for New Zealand Music have to work within limited parameters and focus on only a few musical styles.[5]

Over the past fifty years or so, scholarship on music in Aotearoa/New Zealand has changed vastly. I do not wish to review a large amount of literature on New Zealand music in this introductory chapter, rather, I will address some of the underpinning trends that have been the focus of music research.[6] This is particularly evident in some literature that is intended to represent the nation's soundscape.

A 1966 encyclopaedia entry on music is a useful starting point for discussion, and serves to illustrate which types of music were primarily focussed on in such books. One of the complexities of exploring music in the context of national identity is that one confronts discourses that have established canons and this does much to blurr a true representation of the many musical voices within national boundaries. Take, for instance, *Te Ara—An Encyclopedia of New Zealand*.[7] The entry under "Music" offers some fascinating historical information that provides a sketch of some of the musical activities of New Zealand—but by no means all. The entry begins with a general history, covering such topics as church music, singing, choral societies, visiting companies and musicians, outstanding leaders, academic influences, societies, school music, awards, competitions, orchestras, and broadcasting. While this informative summary of music in New Zealand expresses a sense of a developing national context of music making, there is a distinctly eurocentric (or transnational) emphasis on the types of music being discussed. There is a distinct lack of attention for the musical history of indigenous peoples of Aotearoa/New Zealand, and for that of the many other musical cultures and sub-cultures that contribute to this multicultural musical nation.

New Zealand does, of course, have a history of British colonialism, but, within the bicultural political context, much of the culture transplanted from Europe has developed its own New Zealand identity. New Zealand's National Orchestra was established soon after World War II, and was giving concerts as early as 1947. Many of the players came

---

[5] See http://www.sounz.org.nz.
[6] See also Allan Thomas, *Music in New Zealand: A Reader from the 1940s* (Christchurch: School of Music, University of Canterbury, 2000).
[7] "Music," *Te Ara—The Encyclopedia of New Zealand*, ed. A.H. McLintock, originally published in 1966, updated April 22, 2009, http://www.TeAra.govt.nz/en/1966/music/1.

from established New Zealand families, but, adding to the Europeanization of New Zealand at this time, "other recruits [came] . . . as immigrants from various European countries, bringing with them playing standards that have enhanced the orchestra's quality."[8] The transplanted musical styles of the European courts and their later transformations still dominate the New Zealand soundscape, influencing the repertoire of our various regional orchestras, opera companies, chamber ensembles, and choirs. In this context, it is not always an easy task to identify those musical traits which are distinctly New Zealand, although some composers have explored the sounds of the indigenous peoples of Aotearoa as a way of offering something musical that helped to link music and place. For example:

> Alfred Hill stands alone as the only composer of note in the early period of New Zealand history.[9] Apart from his music, which frequently sought to catch the spirit and flavour of Maoriland, there has been no strongly marked tendency to develop a nationalist school of composition. The most significant composer of recent times is Douglas Lilburn, of Wellington.[10]

Another reference work, *The Oxford History of New Zealand Music*, may be a starting point for music research in some fields, but what it shows is a distinct sense of eurocentrism, ethnocentrism, and cultural imperialism.[11] That said, one of the remarkable things about this book is its introductory chapter by Te Puoho Katene, which is a celebration of Aotearoa/New Zealand's indigenous peoples (albeit this comprises only six pages of a volume of over 300 pages).[12] While a generalized introductory chapter is certainly useful on one level of study, the absence of cultural diversity in a "history of New Zealand music" points to a problematic way of studying music within a nation-state. Acknowledging the limitations of his own work, Thomson notes in his "Introduction" the need to use this history as a starting point for further research: "I hope, nevertheless, that it [the book] will do justice to its subject, will prompt explorations of areas that could only be touched on here and that it will

---

[8] "Music," *Te Ara—The Encyclopedia of New Zealand*.
[9] See further John Mansfield Thomson, *A Distant Music: The Life and Times of Alfred Hill 1870-1960* (Auckland: Oxford University Press, 1980).
[10] Ibid.
[11] John Mansfield Thomson, ed., *The Oxford History of New Zealand Music* (Oxford: Oxford University Press, 1991).
[12] Te Puoho Katene, "The Māori World of Music," in *The Oxford History of New Zealand Music*, ed. John Mansfield Thomson (Oxford: Oxford University Press, 1991), 1–6.

stimulate pride in our musical achievement."[13] The same formulae was also used in Thomson's shorter volume based on the catalogue of an exhibition of the many images held at the Alexander Turnbull Library.[14] Thomson dedicates the first section of this work to traditional Māori music and the impact of European settlement. Later sections explore the themes of colonial musical life, music in performance, and composers at work. As noted in the book's "Preface" by Peter Scott, "the exhibition seeks to chart the emergence of a distinctively New Zealand style of composition and music making."[15]. Scott also notes "the diversity of New Zealand music."[16]

*The New Grove Dictionary of Music and Musicians* is a major reference work in music research. Its "New Zealand" entry offers a refreshing approach to the study of music within a nation's borders. The opening overview of Māori music provides recognition of the indigenous peoples of Aotearoa/New Zealand. Focusing on traditional musical practices, including a number of vocal and instrumental styles, the entry establishes a context for celebrating the partnership of biculturalism as part of the Treaty of Waitangi.[17] The Māori entry is followed by a discussion of European traditional music and western art music. In addition to the recognition of the nation's indigenous peoples, another factor present in this overview of New Zealand music is its acknowledgement of a growing multicultural diversity that is transforming the musical soundscape:

> A variety of minority communities have perpetuated their folk music through clubs and associations. In the North Island popular performers at local events are descendants of 19th-century Bohemian settlers at Puhoi, who maintain a fiddle, accordion and *dudelsack* (bagpipe) band and perform dances such as the Egerlander polka. Similarly, descendants of Dalmatian *kauri* gumfield workers have a *tamburica* orchestra and perform the *kolo*, a traditional circle dance. The cultural activities of other groups, for example Chinese, Indian, Scandinavian, Dutch and Greek communities, and those of British descent (of which the Scots, long associated with pipe

---

[13] Thomson, *The Oxford History of New Zealand Music*, ix.

[14] John Mansfield Thomson, *Musical Images: A New Zealand Historical Journey 1840–1990* (Wellington: National Library of New Zealand/Te Puna Matauranga O Aotearoa, 1990).

[15] Peter Scott, "Preface," in *Musical Images: A New Zealand Historical Journey 1840–1990*, by John Mansfield Thomson (Wellington: National Library of New Zealand/Te Puna Matauranga O Aotearoa, 1990), 7.

[16] Ibid.

[17] Mervyn McLean, Angela R. Annabel, and Adrienne Simpson, "New Zealand," in *Grove Music Online. Oxford Music Online*, http://www.oxfordmusiconline.com/subscriber/article/grove/music/40087.

bands and Highland dancing, have strongly asserted a musical identity) are currently experiencing revitalization in the wake of a large inflow of new Asian residents. In Auckland, New Zealand's largest city, popularly dubbed 'the multicultural capital', an annual Maori and Pacific Islands Secondary Schools' Cultural Festival is expanding to accommodate countries such as China, India, Thailand and Sri Lanka.[18]

Several of the conference papers referred to the biculturalism of Aotearoa/New Zealand with its unique Treaty of Waitangi, although this cultural partnership between Māori and Pākehā is barely represented in the published papers. What became apparent at the conference, and even more so in this publication, was that a small group of scholars cannot represent the nation, nor should they try to. They can simply present knowledge on case-studies that help show historical and contemporary perspectives that contribute to the national whole. That said, the conference recognized that cultural diversity was at the heart of the meeting, and that paper presenters were only going to be able to touch upon a few aspects of a musical nation of peoples, cultures, and individuals.

The present-day context of New Zealand is one of cultural hybridity where there is an interplay between cultures in a postcolonial environment, and interconnection between past and present, each of which serves to contribute to enriching the nation with multifarious musical traditions and identities.[19] It is here that the idea of a singular music and national identity is challenged, and one needs to speak in the plural about musics and

---

[18] Ibid. Compare also *The Garland Encylopedia of World Music*, which has several entries covering the Māori and Pacific musics of Aotearoa/New Zealand: Jan Bolwell, and Keri Kaa, "Māori Dance: An Indigenous View," in *The Garland Encyclopedia of World Music, Australia and the Pacific Islands 9*, ed. Adrienne L. Kaeppler and J.W. Love (New York: Garland Publishing, 1998), 948–51; Te Puoho Katene, "Māori Music," *The Garland Encyclopedia of World Music, Australia and the Pacific Islands 9*, ed. Adrienne L. Kaeppler and J.W. Love (New York: Garland Publishing, 1998), 933–38; Te Ahukaramū Charles Royal, "Mōteatea: Māori Musical Poetry," in *The Garland Encyclopedia of World Music, Australia and the Pacific Islands 9*, ed. Adrienne L. Kaeppler and J.W. Love (New York: Garland Publishing, 1998), 938–44; Amy Ku'uleialoha Stillman, "Aotearoa," in *The Garland Encyclopedia of World Music, Australia and the Pacific Islands 9*, ed. Adrienne L. Kaeppler and J.W. Love (New York: Garland Publishing, 1998), 972–74; Allan Thomas, "Aoteaora," in *The Garland Encyclopedia of World Music, Australia and the Pacific Islands 9*, ed. Adrienne L. Kaeppler and J.W. Love (New York: Garland Publishing, 1998), 928–23.
[19] See, for example, Homi K. Bhabha, *The Location of Culture* (New York: Routledge, 1994).

identies. The boundaries of a nation-state often serve to superimpose a superficial idea of identity, one that can only be understood by looking at the many peoples and individuals who make up that context in the first place. No single book can do this, but this collection of essays attempts to contribute to discourse on the interconnections between identities and musics, and to offer perspectives that help celebrate the cultural diversity of New Zealand's past and present, and the many diverse peoples that live within and beyond its national borders.

In this context, this book attempts to "de-colonize" Aotearoa/New Zealand musical discourse and offer a wider vision of the musical nation and its diverse cultures.[20] As Hebert has observed:

> In New Zealand, music pedagogy has closely followed England, and until recently educational histories have largely emphasized curricular issues rather than cultural ones, while studies of Maori music have traditionally avoided discussion of contemporary hybrid genres in order to emphasize "pre-contact" practices of the distant past.[21]

Like many other countries the world over, New Zealand's colonial past and postcolonial present has created a nation rich in cultural diversity. Having an indigenous Māori population well before European settlers arrived in the eighteenth and nineteenth centuries, influences from Britain and other countries in Europe dominated the nineteenth century and much of the twentieth century, while social and cultural flows from Australia, Polynesia, and Asia have been especially present over the past fifty years. Such is this cultural mix that musical styles reflect both real and perceived heritages, and hybridized forms help create a sense of a unique Aotearoa/New Zealand soundscape.

In this cultural setting, the papers present case-studies of several macro and micro musics. From the perpective of research on people making music, all musical expression is worthy of study. From this viewpoint, the study of music-making is able to offer insight into the sounds of many peoples, cultures, and sub-cultures that have often been neglected in music research. For example, one of the major (ethno-)musicological studies of music making in terms of examining diversity was Ruth Finnegan's study of an English town, which offered fresh insight into how music-making is

---

[20] David G. Hebert, "Rethinking the Historiography of Hybrid Genres in Music Education," in *De-Canonizing Music History*, ed. Vesa Kurkela and Lauri Väkevä (Newcastle: Cambridge Scholars Press, 2009), 163–84.
[21] Ibid., 177.

organized and understood within a small community.[22] Closer to home,
Allan Thomas' "historical ethnography" of Hawera in New Zealand helps
show the extent of cultural heterogeneity in "a relatively remote, small
town" at a brief moment in time.[23] Indeed, in connection with change and
difference in Hawera's musical traditions, values, and differences from the
mid-twentieth centure to the 1990s, Thomas comments that:

> The acceptance and celebration of musical difference relates to a different
> view of society than that held in the decades to mid-century, when such
> differenes were marginalised as quaint or threatening, and musics kept
> apart in separate 'worlds'—the popular music world and the Māori musical
> world.[24]

The conference that was the foundation of this book included topics
that were profoundly diverse and helped show some of the complexities of
trying to locate music in discourses on national identity. What became
apparent during the conference was that the speakers were representing
just a fragment of Aotearoa/New Zealand's many musics, and the fourteen
papers accepted for publication provide just a taste of the diverse musical
practices found within the nation and by its national diaspora.

One of the problems of publishing any book on music and national
identity is the fact that it is going to be extremely difficult, if not
impossible, to represent everyone living in the nation-state. While the lack
of insider representation of Māori music and various micro, migrant, and
transcultural musics of Aotearoa/New Zealand is certainly acknowledged
as a lacuna in this book, it should be emphasized that as a collection of
papers that were originally presented as part of a conference, the final
manuscript was dependent on a number of factors including representation
at the conference, submission of papers for the publication, and acceptance
of papers. There are, however, very few scholarly works that engage with

---

[22] Ruth Finnegan, *The Hidden Musicians: Music-making in an English Town*
(Cambridge: Cambridge University Press, 1989).
[23] Allan Thomas, *Music is Where You Find it: Music in the Town of Hawera, 1946.
An Historical Ethnography* (Wellington: Music Books New Zealand, 2004), 14.
[24] Ibid., 182. On other types of more recent popular music that have become the
subject of scholarly discussion, see John Dix, *Stranded in Paradise: New Zealand
Rock'n'roll 1955–88* (Palmerston North: Paradise Publications, 1988); David
Eggleton, *Ready to Fly: The Story of New Zealand Rock Music* (Nelson: Craig
Potton Publishing, 2003); Tony Mitchell, "Kia Kaha! (Be Strong!): Maori and
Pacific Islander Hip-hop in Aotearoa-New Zealand," in *Global Noise: Rap and
Hip-Hop Outside the USA*, ed. Tony Mitchell (Middletown: Wesleyan University
Press, 2001), 280–305.

the musics of Māori cultures in comparison to other indigenous musics of the world.[25] The summaries and analyses offered by McLean and others help contribute to discourse in this field of music-making, and the many other musics of New Zealand, apart from western art, are seldom discussed in pre-twenty-first century ethnomusicological or musicological scholarship of New Zealand music.[26] In this context, the intention of this

---

[25] Many relevant works by McLean and others on Māori music are listed in the Bibliography. See also the work of Johannes C. Andersen, "An Introduction to Maori Music," *Transactions of the New Zealand Institute* 54 (1923): 743–62; Johannes C. Andersen, "Maori Musical Instruments," *Art in New Zealand* 2 (1929): 91–101; Johannes C. Andersen, *Maori Music with its Polynesian Background* (New Plymouth: Thomas Avery & Sons, 1934); Elsdon Best, "The Maori," *Memoirs of the Polynesian Society* 5 (1924); Elsdon Best, "Games and Pastimes of the Maori: An Account of Various Exercises, Games and Pastimes of the Natives of New Zealand, as Practised in Former Times; Including Some Information Concerning Their Vocal and Instrumental Music," *Dominion Museum Bulletin, Wellington* 8 (1925); Elsdon Best, *Tuhoe: The Children of the Mist. A Sketch of the Origin, History, Myths and Beliefs of the Tuhoe Tribes of the Maori of New Zealand; With Some Account of Other Early Tribes of the Bay of Plenty District* (New Plymouth: Thomas Avery & Sons, 1925); Keith Kennedy, "The Ancient Four-Note Musical Scale of the Maoris," *Mankind* 1 (1931): 11–14; Hirini Melbourne, *Toiapiapi: He Huinga o Ngā Kura Pūoro a te Māori* (Te Whanganui a Tara, Titi Tuhiwai, 1993); Hirini Melbourne and Richard Nunns, *Te Ku Te Whe*, RAT-D004, 1994; Apirana Ngata, *Ngā Mōteatea. The Songs. Scattered Pieces From Many Canoe Areas, Part 1* (Wellington: A.H. & A.W. Reed, 1928); Apirana Ngata, *Ngā Mōteatea. The Songs. Scattered Pieces From Many Canoe Areas, Part 2*, Translated by Pei Te Hurinui (Wellington: A.H. & A.W. Reed, 1961); Apirana Ngata, *Ngā Mōteatea. The Songs. Scattered Pieces From Many Canoe Areas. Part 3*, Translated by Pei Te Hurinui (Wellington: A.H. & A.W. Reed, 1970); Apirana Ngata, *Ngā Mōteatea. The Songs. Scattered Pieces From Many Canoe Areas, Part 4* (Wellington: A.H. & A.W. Reed, 1990); Jennifer Shennan, *The Maori Action Song: Waiata a Ringa, Waiata Kori, no Whea Tenei Ahua Hou?* (Wellington: New Zealand Council for Educational Research, 1984); Suzanne Youngerman,. "Maori Dancing Since the Eighteenth Century," *Ethnomusicology* 18, no. 1 (1974): 75–100. Cf. D.R. Harvey, *A Bibliography of Writings about New Zealand Music, Published to the End of 1983* (Wellington: Victoria University Press, 1985); Henry Johnson, "Indigenous Musics of Aotearoa/New Zealand: An Exploration of Early Observations, Attitudes, and Perspectives in the Historical Narratives of Ethnomusicological Scholarship, *British Review of New Zealand Studies* 12 (2000): 113-30; Maureen Stewart, *Maori Music: An Annotated Bibliography* (Wellington: Library School, 1969).

[26] See Dan Bendrups, "A Cultural History of the Christchurch Latvian Choir," in *Music on the Edge: Select Proceedings of the 2007 IASPM-ANZ Conference*, ed. Dan Bendrups (Dunedin: IAPSM-ANZ, 2008), 9–14; David G.Hebert, "Music

book is to open up critical discourse on the many musics (voices) of Aotearoa/New Zealand. The chapters presented herein represent just a few sounds of a diverse nation, and sounds that do much to represent place, very often Aotearoa/New Zealand and beyond.

This collection of essays is divided into three parts which relate to overarching themes of the book: (1) Cultural Diversity; (2) Popular Culture; and (3) Education and High-Art. Part 1 breaks away from the notion of a dominant music culture in a bicultural political milieu with the aim of identifying and celebrating some of the many musical voices that can be heard in Aotearoa/New Zealand. Tony Mitchell, the keynote speaker at the conference, opens the collection by problematizing the term

---

Transculturation and Identity in a Maori Brass Band Tradition," *Alta Musica* 26 (2008): 173–200; David G. Hebert, "Music Transmission in an Auckland Tongan Community Youth Band," *International Journal of Community Music* 1, no. 2 (2008): 169–88; Henry Johnson, "Indigenous Musics of Aotearoa/New Zealand;" Henry Johnson, "Performing Identity, Past and Present: Chinese Cultural Performance, New Year Celebrations, and the Heritage Industry," in *East by South: China in the Australasian Imagination*, ed. Charles Ferrall, Paul Millar and Keren Smith (Wellington: Victoria University Press, 2005), 217–42; Henry Johnson, "Striking Accord! Gamelan, Education, and Indonesian Cultural Flows in Aotearoa/New Zealand," in *Asia in the Making of New Zealand*, ed. Henry Johnson and Brian Moloughney (Auckland: Auckland University Press, 2006), 185–203; Henry Johnson, "'Happy Diwali!': Performance, Multicultural Soundscapes and Intervention in Aotearoa/New Zealand," in *Musical Performance in the Diaspora*, ed. Tina K. Ramnarine (New York: Routledge, 2007), 71–94; Henry Johnson, "Composing Asia in New Zealand: Gamelan and Creativity," *New Zealand Journal of Asian Studies* 10, no. 1 (2008): 54–84; Henry Johnson, "Partnerships, Multicultural Music Education, and New Zealand's Asian Communities," *Sound Ideas* 7 (2008): 19–26; Henry Johnson, "Why *Taiko*? Understanding *Taiko* Performance at New Zealand's 1st *Taiko* Festival," *Sites. A Journal of Social Anthropology and Cultural Studies* 5, no. 2 (2008): 111–34; Henry Johnson, "Musical Moves and Transnational Grooves: Education, Transplantation and Japanese *Taiko* Drumming at The International Pacific College, New Zealand," in *Recentring Asia: Histories, Encounters, Identities*, ed. Jacob Edmond, Henry Johnson, and Jacqueline Leckie (Folkestone: Global Oriental), in press; Henry Johnson, with Guil Figgins, "Diwali Downunder: Transforming and Performing Indian Tradition in Aotearoa/New Zealand," in *Sociology of Diaspora: A Reader*, ed. Ajaya Kumar Sahoo and Brij Maharaj (Jaipur: Rawat Publications, 2007), 913–39; Benjamin Le Heux, "An Investigative and Documentary Study of Music and Change Within a Buddhist Community in Christchurch, New Zealand" (M.A. diss., University of Canterbury, 2002); Siong Ngor Ng, "The Chinese Community in Auckland: A Musical Ethnography and Musical History" (M.A. diss., University of Auckland, 2000).

"Kiwi music" in the context of denoting Aotearoa/New Zealand national identity in music. With various examples from the popular music scene, Mitchell offers an overview of some of the sounds that might be called Kiwi, while challenging notions of New Zealandness in this sphere of music-making. In his paper on migrant music in New Zealand, Dan Bendrups brings the discussion to some of the many micro musics that seldom, if ever, make the topics of scholarly debate. While grounding his work in broader migrant and diaspora discourses, Bendrups provides several case-studies of ethnicity and identity that help show the richness of Aotearoa/New Zealand's musical diversity. Three further papers in Part 1 also contribute to this discourse. In her research on Wellington's Cuba Street Carnival, Shelley Brunt writes about this showcase of musical diversity in New Zealand which celebrates Wellington's many cultural groups. As one of a multitude of music or music-related festivals in New Zealand, the Cuba Street Carnival, Brunt suggests, is a setting where ideas of cultural identity and place provide themes for a wider understanding of the nation's multifarious music-making. My own paper in this collection focuses on one genre of music that has increasingly become more popular among several of New Zealand's many ethnicities: Japanese *taiko* (drum) performance. The paper aims to understand what it means to be a *taiko* player in New Zealand, regardless of ethnicity. The final paper in Part 1 is Alison Booth's examination of the role academics have in producing events in the world music scene. In her paper, Booth maps out five major events over a ten-year period that involved visiting performers contributing to a broader New Zealand music scene, which ultimately helped to influence local identity.

Part 2 focuses on popular culture. Kirsten Zemke offers a study of music, identity, and cultural diversity in an Auckland suburb based on an original musical theatre production: *Our Street*. Zemke was musical director and composer for the show, which included an array of local talent. In her paper, Zemke argues that *Our Street* "negotiated multiple layers, journeys, and cultural political transactions" in a production that utilized local and global music and helped express and construct identity for all involved. Matthew Bannister's contribution to this collection is a case-study on Bic Runga, who quickly became an Aotearoa/New Zealand icon in the popular music industry. Bannister offers a discussion of Runga's representations in her music and videos in the context of "Kiwi" identity construction where "non-white females are doubly marginalized." The next two papers offer perspectives on jazz culture in Aotearoa/New Zealand. Aleisha Ward's paper explores the construction of a local jazz culture in connection with Australian, American, and British jazz influences from the 1920s to the 1950s. At a time of changing relationships, Ward shows how jazz culture was constructed through a process of cultural negotiation with the international jazz scene of these countries. The focus of Norman Meehan's paper is Mike Nock, one of the country's leading jazz performers. Meehan explores Nock's contribution to the Aotearoa/New Zealand's jazz scene with particular reference to the performer's place as a local artist producing a New Zealand sound. The final essay in this part is by Andy Gibson, who provides a linguistic analysis of identity in New Zealand popular music. Gibson's emphasis is on vowel differences between singing and speaking.

Three papers comprise Part 3. The first is on education, where Sally Bodkin-Allen provides a case-study of national identity in the *Kiwi Kidsongs* series of books for use in primary music education. Bodkin-Allen's argument is that national identity is both created and represented in this series of music, something that shows state-funded influence helping to nurture a sense of identity among young children. Two papers are offered on New Zealand's western high-art music scene. Robin Maconie's paper is a study of prehistory in New Zealand music, suggesting some links between Māori music and European high-art music. The final paper is by Marian Poole, who explores the place, background, and influences of early twentieth-century art music on Aotearoa/New Zealand.

As a way of closing the book, Graeme Downes provides a paper that questions national identity: who wants to know and why? Downes provokes the reader to think about ideas pertaining to national identity, especially in a contemporary context where Aotearoa/New Zealand increasingly looks to the wider world in an age of ever-increasing global flows and influences.

This collection of essays provides a starting point to re-think music and national identity in Aotearoa/New Zealand. The papers offer various perspectives on the interconnections between music and identity, while offering case-studies on diverse topics including specific performers, composers, musical styles, and events. The papers cannot cover everything and, as I have pointed out above, they simply "scratch the surface." However, what they can offer will hopefully open up further research on the many voices of those who call Aotearoa/New Zealand home.

# References

Andersen, Johannes C. "An Introduction to Maori Music." *Transactions of the New Zealand Institute* 54 (1923): 743–62.

—. "Maori Musical Instruments." *Art in New Zealand* 2 (1929): 91–101.

—. *Maori Music with its Polynesian Background*. New Plymouth: Thomas Avery & Sons, 1934.

Bendrups, Dan. "A Cultural History of the Christchurch Latvian Choir." In *Music on the Edge: Select Proceedings of the 2007 IASPM-ANZ Conference*, edited by Dan Bendrups, 9–14. Dunedin: IAPSM-ANZ, 2008.

Best, Elsdon. "The Maori." *Memoirs of the Polynesian Society* 5 (1924).

—. "Games and Pastimes of the Maori: An Account of Various Exercises, Games and Pastimes of the Natives of New Zealand, as Practised in Former Times; Including Some Information Concerning Their Vocal and Instrumental Music." *Dominion Museum Bulletin, Wellington* 8 (1925).

—. *Tuhoe: The Children of the Mist. A Sketch of the Origin, History, Myths and Beliefs of the Tuhoe Tribes of the Maori of New Zealand; With Some Account of Other Early Tribes of the Bay of Plenty District.* New Plymouth: Thomas Avery & Sons, 1925.

Bhabha, Homi K. *The Location of Culture*. New York: Routledge, 1994.

Bolwell, Jan, and Keri Kaa. "Māori Dance: An Indigenous View." In *The Garland Encyclopedia of World Music, Australia and the Pacific Islands 9*, edited by Adrienne L. Kaeppler and J.W. Love, 948–51. New York: Garland Publishing, 1998.

Cheng, Derek, Simon Collins, and Wayne Thompson. "We Need a New Flag it's Time For a Change." *New Zealand Herald*, February 4, 2010, http://www.knowledge-basket.co.nz.

Dix, John. *Stranded in Paradise: New Zealand Rock'n'roll 1955–88*. Palmerston North: Paradise Publications, 1988.

Eggleton, David. *Ready to Fly: The Story of New Zealand Rock Music*. Nelson: Craig Potton Publishing, 2003.

Finnegan, Ruth. *The Hidden Musicians: Music-making in an English Town*. Cambridge: Cambridge University Press, 1989.

Hall, Stuart. "Cultural Identity and Diaspora." In *Identity: Community, Culture, Difference*, edited by Jonathan Rutherford, 222–37. London: Lawrence & Wishart, 1990.

Harvey, D.R. *A Bibliography of Writings about New Zealand Music, Published to the End of 1983*. Wellington: Victoria University Press, 1985.

Hebert, David G. "Music Transculturation and Identity in a Maori Brass Band Tradition." *Alta Musica* 26 (2008): 173–200.

—. "Music Transmission in an Auckland Tongan Community Youth Band." *International Journal of Community Music* 1, no. 2 (2008): 169–88.

—. "Rethinking the Historiography of Hybrid Genres in Music Education." In *De-Canonizing Music History*, edited by Vesa Kurkela and Lauri Väkevä, 163–84. Newcastle: Cambridge Scholars Press, 2009.

Johnson, Henry. "Indigenous Musics of Aotearoa/New Zealand: An Exploration of Early Observations, Attitudes, and Perspectives in the Historical Narratives of Ethnomusicological Scholarship. *British Review of New Zealand Studies* 12 (2000): 113-30.

—. "Performing Identity, Past and Present: Chinese Cultural Performance, New Year Celebrations, and the Heritage Industry." In *East by South: China in the Australasian Imagination*, edited by Charles Ferrall, Paul Millar, and Keren Smith, 217–42. Wellington: Victoria University Press, 2005.

—. "Striking Accord! Gamelan, Education, and Indonesian Cultural Flows in Aotearoa/New Zealand." In *Asia in the Making of New Zealand*, edited by Henry Johnson and Brian Moloughney, 185–203. Auckland: Auckland University Press, 2006.

—. "'Happy Diwali!': Performance, Multicultural Soundscapes and Intervention in Aotearoa/New Zealand." In *Musical Performance in the Diaspora*, edited by Tina K. Ramnarine, 71–94. New York: Routledge, 2007.

—. "Composing Asia in New Zealand: Gamelan and Creativity." *New Zealand Journal of Asian Studies* 10, no. 1 (2008): 54–84.

—. "Partnerships, Multicultural Music Education, and New Zealand's Asian Communities." *Sound Ideas* 7 (2008): 19–26.

—. "Why *Taiko*? Understanding *Taiko* Performance at New Zealand's 1st *Taiko* Festival." *Sites. A Journal of Social Anthropology and Cultural Studies* 5, no. 2 (2008): 111–34.

—. "Musical Moves and Transnational Grooves: Education, Transplantation and Japanese *Taiko* Drumming at The International Pacific College, New Zealand." In *Recentring Asia: Histories, Encounters, Identities*, edited by Jacob Edmond, Henry Johnson, and Jacqueline Leckie. Folkestone: Global Oriental, in press.

—. With Guil Figgins. "Diwali Downunder: Transforming and Performing Indian Tradition in Aotearoa/New Zealand." In *Sociology of Diaspora: A Reader*, edited by Ajaya Kumar Sahoo and Brij Maharaj, 913–39. Jaipur: Rawat Publications, 2007.

Katene, Te Puoho. "The Māori World of Music." In *The Oxford History of New Zealand Music*, edited by John Mansfield Thomson, 1–6. Oxford: Oxford University Press, 1991.

—. "Māori Music." *The Garland Encyclopedia of World Music, Australia and the Pacific Islands 9*, edited by Adrienne L. Kaeppler and J.W. Love, 933–38. New York: Garland Publishing, 1998.

Kennedy, Keith. "The Ancient Four-Note Musical Scale of the Maoris." *Mankind* 1 (1931): 11–14.

Le Heux, Benjamin. "An Investigative and Documentary Study of Music and Change Within a Buddhist Community in Christchurch, New Zealand." M.A. diss., University of Canterbury, 2002.

McLean, Mervyn. "Field Work in Maori Music: Preliminary Study." M.A. diss., University of Otago, 1958.

—. "Oral Transmission in Maori Music." *Journal of the International Folk Music Council* 13 (1961): 59–62.

—. "A Preliminary Analysis of 87 Maori Chants." *Ethnomusicology* 8, no.1 (1964): 41–48.

—. "Maori Chant: A Study in Ethnomusicology." Ph.D. diss., University of Otago, 1965.

—. "A New Method of Melodic Interval Analysis as Applied to Maori Chant." *Ethnomusicology* 10, no. 2 (1966): 174–90.

—. "An Investigation of the Open Tube Maori Flute or Kooauau." *Journal of the Polynesian Society* 77, no. 3 (1968): 213–41.

—. "An Analysis of 651 Maori Scales." *Yearbook of the International Folk Music Council* 1 (1969): 123–64.

—. "The New Zealand Nose Flute: Fact or Fallacy?" *The Galpin Society Journal* 27 (1974): 79–94.

—. "Towards the Differentiation of Music Areas in Oceania." *Anthropos* 74 (1979): 717–36.

—. "Unesco 'World History of Music' Proposal: The Case for Field Research in Oceania." *Bulletin of the International Committee on Urgent Anthropological and Ethnological Research* 21 (1979): 99–113.

—. "A Chronological and Geographical Sequence of Maori Flute Scales." *Man* 17 (1982): 123–57.

—. *Catalogue of Radio New Zealand Recordings of Maori Events 1938–1950*. Auckland: Archive of Maori and Pacific Music, 1991.

—. "Oceania." In *Ethnomusicology: Historical and Regional Studies*, edited Helen Myers, 392–400. London: Macmillan, 1993.

—. *An Annotated Bibliography of Oceania Music and Dance*. Revised and enlarged second edition. Michigan: Harmonie Park Press, [1977, 1981] 1995.

—. *Catalogue of Maori Purposes Fund Board Recordings Recorded by W.T. Ngata 1953–58*. Auckland: Archive of Maori and Pacific Music, [1983] 1995.

—. *Maori Music*. Auckland: Auckland University Press, 1996.

—. *Weavers of Song: Polynesian Music and Dance*. Auckland: Auckland University Press, 1999.

McLean, Mervyn, Angela R. Annabel, and Adrienne Simpson. "New Zealand." In *Grove Music Online. Oxford Music Online*, http://www.oxfordmusiconline.com/subscriber/article/grove/music/400 87.

McLean, Mervyn, and Jeny Curnow, eds. *Catalogue of McLean Collection Recordings of Traditional Maori Songs, 1958–79*. Auckland: Archive of Maori and Pacific Music, 1992.

McLean, Mervyn, and Jeny Curnow, eds. *Catalogue of Museum of New Zealand Cylinder Recordings of Traditional Māori Songs, 1919–c1935*. Auckland: Archive of Maori and Pacific Music, University of Auckland, 1992.

McLean, Mervyn, and Margaret Orbell. *Traditional Songs of the Maori*. Revised edition. Auckland: Auckland University Press, [1975] 1990.

Melbourne, Hirini. *Toiapiapi: He Huinga o Ngā Kura Pūoro a te Māori*. Te Whanganui a Tara, Titi Tuhiwai, 1993.

Melbourne, Hirini, and Richard Nunns. *Te Ku Te Whe*. RAT-D004, 1994.

Mitchell, Tony. "Kia Kaha! (Be Strong!): Maori and Pacific Islander Hip-hop in Aotearoa-New Zealand." In *Global Noise: Rap and Hip-Hop Outside the USA*, edited by Tony Mitchell, 280–305. Middletown: Wesleyan University Press, 2001.

Ng, Siong Ngor. "The Chinese Community in Auckland: A Musical Ethnography and Musical History." M.A. diss., University of Auckland, 2000.

Ngata, Apirana. *Ngā Mōteatea. The Songs. Scattered Pieces From Many Canoe Areas, Part 1*. Wellington: A.H. & A.W. Reed, 1928.

—. *Ngā Mōteatea. The Songs. Scattered Pieces From Many Canoe Areas, Part 2*. Translated by Pei Te Hurinui. Wellington: A.H. & A.W. Reed, 1961.

—. *Ngā Mōteatea. The Songs. Scattered Pieces From Many Canoe Areas. Part 3*, Translated by Pei Te Hurinui. Wellington: A.H. & A.W. Reed, 1970.

—. *Ngā Mōteatea. The Songs. Scattered Pieces From Many Canoe Areas, Part 4*. Wellington: A.H. & A.W. Reed, 1990.

Royal, Te Ahukaramū Charles. "Mōteatea: Māori Musical Poetry." In *The Garland Encyclopedia of World Music, Australia and the Pacific Islands 9*, edited by Adrienne L. Kaeppler and J.W. Love, 938–44. New York: Garland Publishing, 1998.

Scott, Peter. "Preface." In *Musical Images: A New Zealand Historical Journey 1840–1990*, by John Mansfield Thomson. Wellington: National Library of New Zealand/Te Puna Matauranga O Aotearoa, 1990.

Shennan, Jennifer. *The Maori Action Song: Waiata a Ringa, Waiata Kori, no Whea Tenei Ahua Hou?* Wellington: New Zealand Council for Educational Research, 1984.

Slobin, Mark, *Subcultural Sounds: Micromusics of the West*. Hanover: University Press of New England, 1993.

Stewart, Maureen. *Maori Music: An Annotated Bibliography*. Wellington: Library School, 1969.

Stillman, Amy Ku'uleialoha. "Aotearoa." In *The Garland Encyclopedia of World Music, Australia and the Pacific Islands 9*, edited by Adrienne L. Kaeppler and J.W. Love, 972–74. New York: Garland Publishing, 1998.

*Te Ara—Encyclopedia of New Zealand, An*. Edited by A.H. McLintock, originally published in 1966, updated April 22, 2009, http://www.TeAra.govt.nz/en/1966/music/1.

Thomas, Allan. "Aoteaora." In *The Garland Encyclopedia of World Music, Australia and the Pacific Islands 9*, edited by Adrienne L. Kaeppler and J.W. Love, 928–23. New York: Garland Publishing, 1998.

—. *Music in New Zealand: A Reader from the 1940s*. Christchurch: School of Music, University of Canterbury, 2000.

—. *Music is Where You Find it: Music in the Town of Hawera, 1946. An Historical Ethnography*. Wellington: Music Books New Zealand, 2004.

Thomson, John Mansfield. *A Distant Music: The Life and Times of Alfred Hill 1870-1960*. Auckland: Oxford University Press, 1980.

—. *Musical Images: A New Zealand Historical Journey 1840–1990*. Wellington: National Library of New Zealand/Te Puna Matauranga O Aotearoa, 1990.

—. *The Oxford History of New Zealand Music*. Oxford: Oxford University Press, 1991.

Youngerman, Suzanne. "Maori Dancing Since the Eighteenth Century." *Ethnomusicology* 18, no. 1 (1974): 75–100.

# PART I:

# CULTURAL DIVERSITY

CHAPTER TWO

"KIWI" MUSIC AND NEW ZEALAND
NATIONAL IDENTITY

TONY MITCHELL

As Graeme Downes noted in his abstract for the conference from
which this book is derived, it is important to "render notions of national
identity problematic or discomforting" in the interests of avoiding the
homogenization of diverse expressions of place and identity, and
inappropriate expressions of jingoistic patriotism. The term "Kiwi music"
is an example of a term often used to denote New Zealand national
identity in music, and one which needs problematizing. It is also an
indicator of what Downes calls "prescribed and comfortable notions of
national identity" which are usually fixed and stereotypically exclusive,
rather than accommodating important aspects of indigeneity and changing
patterns of migration.

   In 2007, I was asked to contribute an entry on "Kiwi rock" to the
*Encyclopedia of Popular Music of the World*. I agreed on the condition
that I could re-title it "New Zealand rock." It seems a small distinction, but
the term "Kiwi" has become something of an easy, lazy marker of New
Zealandness that has a predominantly Pākehā cast, and which not only
does not usually acknowledge Māori identities, but excludes the numerous
other hyphenated identities which exist in Aotearoa/New Zealand. The NZ
On Air series *Kiwi Hit Discs*, a monthly selection of tracks for radio play
featuring popular New Zealand musicians, is arguably an example of this
rather jingoistic use of the term applied to music. Granted, the series also
includes occasional instalments of Māori music called "Iwi Hit Discs,"
which looks suspiciously as if "iwi" is being subsumed into "Kiwi"—just
because it rhymes doesn't make it any more palatable. The radio station
Kiwi FM prides itself on playing only New Zealand music, but DJs rarely
back-announce or identify what they play, a frustrating omission which
almost seems to defeat the station's purpose. The distinction between
nationally-defined forms of music and radically self-determining expressions

of music produced in "outsider" New Zealand music (such as Coco Solid's "half caste" hip hop, to use just one of numerous examples), which have a much more artistic and incisive connection to New Zealand topographies, finds resonances in the militant Māori hip hop of Te Kupu, who has used film as well as music to explore extensively his alliances with indigenous and minority hip hop communities throughout the world. In an interview I did with him in Sydney in 2007, he addressed the issue of Kiwi-ism:

> Why are we called Kiwis? Why are you so proud of being a Kiwi? Can't you be Māori? Unless they're not all Māori, but just Kiwi things, just those ideologies, philosophical things that I see being pushed around. I'm so wary of this Kiwism . . . that national identity that everyone's a Kiwi. People that come from overseas, from Iraq perhaps, or Afghanistan, if they come to the country: 'If you're gonna live here, you gotta be a Kiwi' . . . What is that? We're gonna be Māori, man, we're not no Kiwis. But the majority of Māori people call themselves Kiwis. They've been brainwashed into this Kiwi mentality, which is the mainstream mentality.[1]

This complacent concept of a mainstream Kiwism also resonates with a statement made on the New Zealand Experimental Poetry website by Lyttleton-based noise musician Bruce Russell, a long-time member of the Dead C, an experimental music group with arguably more of an international profile than a national one:

> There's this thing called 'kiwi' music and it's not the same as New Zealand music. The kind of music that's being sold to New Zealand as a cultural expression [is what's] acceptable to commercial radio programmers. That baldly is how it works. I'm not saying that's wrong and ought never to be done, but somebody's got to be prepared to put a bit of money towards people who are prepared to do things for artistic reasons.[2]

This reading of "Kiwi music" as narrowly commercial further resonates with a highly reductive 1994 article by Roy Shuker and Michael Pickering entitled "Kiwi Rock: Popular Music and Cultural Identity in New Zealand"—a title already indicative of a homogenization of the diversity of New Zealand music into one amorphous, synthetic genre, "Kiwi rock." Here the authors dismiss most New Zealand music before the 1990s as

---

[1] Te Kupu, interview by author, October 2007.
[2] Bruce Russell, "Biography," *NZ Electronic Poetry Centre Website*, http://www.nzepc.auckland.ac.nz.

"local versions of overseas genres and idioms,"[3] and endorse the cultural imperialist argument of Geoff Lealand who, in a 1988 book entitled *A Foreign Egg in Our Nest?*, claims that "all New Zealand music . . . is derivative. It borrows from abroad, expanding on imported influences, denying them, and then re-embracing them. Styles, themes and sounds are all borrowed."[4]

This misguidedly literal search for reflections of aspects of national cultural identity in New Zealand popular music excludes any Māori or Pacific Island music, due to Shuker's and Pickering's lack of knowledge or cultural credentials, and mostly reflects their sketchy knowledge of other New Zealand music. The authors first target the New Zealand music of the 1950s, when, of course, cover versions of US rock'n'roll songs predominated; then the 1960s, which they dismiss as merely following the British beat era—something I'm sure Rim D. Paul would have something to say about, given the proliferation of Māori and Pacific Island music in that era, especially as featured in John O'Shea's film *Don't Let It Get You*,[5] which is overdue for rehabilitation. Shot in Rotorua in 1966 with Howard Morrison, Herma Keil, the Quin Tikis, Rim D. Paul, Lew Pryme, and Australian singer Normie Rowe, it was crammed full of indigenous performers, including, most notably, Kiri Te Kanawa singing a Rossini aria inside a Māori meeting house. In his recent book on New Zealand cinema, which includes an analysis of O'Shea's film, Bruce Babington suggests that the local music scene of the mid-1960s was "dominated by Māori and Polynesian performers, whose talent the film showcases."[6]

Shuker and Pickering go on to reduce the culturally distinctive Flying Nun bands of the 1980s to clones of The Velvet Underground and The Smiths (a group only formed in 1982). For Shuker and Pickering, New Zealand rock music up to the 1990s, at least, presents a case of "imitation stifling the development of a distinctively local sound," and they attempt to illustrate this thesis by demonstrating that there is little evidence of national indicators in band names, song lyrics, the use of New Zealand accents or distinctive stylistic musical idioms.[7] Leaving aside the widespread use of Māori *waiata* and other musical elements, and the

---

[3] Roy Shuker and Michael Pickering, "Kiwi Rock; Popular Music and Cultural Identity in New Zealand," *Popular Music* 13, no. 3 (1994): 270–71, 281.
[4] Geoff Lealand, *A Foreign Egg in Our Nest?* (Wellington: Victoria University Press, 1988), 75.
[5] *Don't Let It Get You*, Film, John O'Shea (Wellington: Pacific Films, 1966).
[6] Bruce Babington, *A History of the New Zealand Fiction Feature Film* (Manchester: Manchester University Press, 2007), 104.
[7] Shuker and Pickering, "Kiwi Rock," 273.

"pacific strum" in much New Zealand music, apart from emphasizing that the relationship between music, place, and identity is far more than simply one of literal place name reference (rather an imaginative and relational inscription of place through networks and milieus of music production, venues, infrastructures and local music practices, scenes and communities as well as social, political, and cultural perspective), it is also important to distinguish between imitation and influence.[8]

Local bands of the 1960s may have begun playing the repertoires of "British Invasion" groups as covers (as did Chants R'n'B in Christchurch, Grim Ltd. in Palmerston North, The Third Chapter in Dunedin, and The Unknown Blues in Invercargill), but most developed their own musical direction subsequently or else faded from view, leaving their distinctive mark on local music histories in the process. Strong indicators of a local, and especially regional, identity in New Zealand music—whether the compositions are original or not—have always been evident in the performance of the music, in the interstices between the texts and musical and lyrical idioms of songs and their reception by audiences, as well in the music's extra-musical contexts such as dress, environment, visual styles, and imagery, as well as social rituals. They are also present in the nature of the music itself—individual ways of playing, performing, and singing that go far beyond simply imitating overseas influences and relate to creating affective relationships with listeners and audiences. The La De Das' 1966 song "How Is the Air Up There?" (which Shuker and Pickering reduce to a Blues Magoos cover by a band sounding like The Rolling Stones), in actual fact had significant purchase among local audiences in Auckland and elsewhere as a locally-produced "alternative" hit song, and even became the title of a later K-Tel compilation of 1960s New Zealand songs, as well as a catchphrase applied generally to 1960s rock music in New Zealand.[9]

While Shuker and Pickering attempt to "cut down to size" any potential for original, geomorphic, or locally distinctive music in New Zealand, their emphasis on national rather than local or regional identity

---

[8] See John Street, "(Dis)located? Rhetoric, Politics, Meaning and the Locality," in *Popular Music: Style and Identity,* ed. Will Straw et al. (Montreal: Centre for Research on Canadian Cultural Industries and Institutions, 1995), 255–63.

[9] See Michael Flint, "What the Air Was Like Up There: Overseas Music and Local Reception in the 1960s," in *North Meets South: Popular Music in Aotearoa/New Zealand,* ed. Philip Hayward, Tony Mitchell and Roy Shuker (Sydney: Perfect Beat Publications, 1994), 1–15; Nina Herriman, "The Air Down Here: Global and Local Interpretations of New Zealand Popular Music, 1955–1977" (M.A. diss., University of Auckland, 2004).

has implications which are dealt with in John Street's comments about local and national music:

> While the business of being recognised entails becoming linked to the national scene, this does not mean that the local becomes completely submerged. Indeed, it is central to the process that a sense of difference be retained. What is to be recognised is what makes the locality different. Indeed, the local is defined against the national. Or, to put it another way, the national is being cut down to size.[10]

Neil Finn's controversial attempt in May 2007 to "cut down to size" national definitions of New Zealand music,[11] and the often virulently exclusionist and nationalistic debate which followed, are a case in point. Criticizing Helen Clark for comparing New Zealand Music Month to Anzac Day and Waitangi Day, and for taking undue credit for the achievements of New Zealand music, as well as NZ on Air's financing of New Zealand music as generating unrealistic expectations of overseas success, Finn was arguably also criticizing the nationalistic jingoism surrounding much of the government support and promotion of Kiwi music. Finn himself has a strong affective connection to Auckland and the North Island of New Zealand, and his song "Kare Kare" celebrates a psychogeographic attachment to the eponymous beach on the west coast of Auckland, which houses a recording studio where Crowded House's album *Together Alone* was recorded.[12]
Nonetheless, his is arguably a local and transnational alliance rather than an expression of any national or "Kiwi" identity. He may have worn a badge of a kiwi on his shirt during Crowded House's "Farewell to the World" concert at the Sydney Opera House in 1996, but this could be read as an example of "strategic essentialism"; distinguishing himself from the Australian members of the band and the audience, and appealing to New Zealand expatriates in Sydney. Indeed, Crowded House has always been something of a transnational band, and now, with two US members, one Australian, and Neil Finn, they have few remnants of New Zealand identity beyond Finn's distinctive presence as their main singer-songwriter.

---

[10] Street, "(Dis)located? Rhetoric, Politics, Meaning and the Locality," 260.
[11] Ibid.
[12] Crowded House, *Together Alone*, Capitol Records 7243 8 27048 2 2, 1993. Tony Mitchell, "The Sounds of Nowhere? Bicultural Music in Aotearoa/New Zealand," in *Popular Music and Local Identity: Rock, Pop and Rap in Europe and Oceania*, ed. Tony Mitchell (London: Leicester University Press, 1996), 222.

Like Crowded House, much of the music produced in Aotearoa is transnational and translocal, as opposed to derivative and borrowed in its representations of place and locality, insofar as it expresses what Doreen Massey has called "articulated movements in networks of social relations and understandings."[13] Massey defines four aspects of a dynamic and progressive sense of place: as interactions and processes rather than fixed entities; as linkages to the outside rather than confined by boundaries, enclosures and divisions; as containing internal conflicts and multiple identities rather than single identities; and as reproducing a specificity that is not bound by an internalized history. As a result, we can entertain "a sense of place which is extroverted, which includes a consciousness of its links with the wider world, which integrates in a positive way the global and the local."[14] As a transnational musician with an Australasian and global identity, Neil Finn embodies this expansive sense of situatedness between places which expresses multiple identities rather than narrow, fixed confinements of the national. On a more superficial level, Kiwi FM advertises itself as "New Zealand's global radio station—now available in Cape Reinga" (the northernmost point of the country), despite its very small listenership; while Saatchi and Saatchi has marketed the slogan "world famous in New Zealand" in relation to Lemon & Paeroa, the "local" soft drink now owned by Coca Cola/Schweppes. The Saatchi and Saatchi slogan has also been adopted as the title of a number of compilations of New Zealand popular music. There is a sense of irony contained in what Keam refers to as "the self contradiction embedded in the advertizing slogan, which teases us in our determination to be noticed."[15]

Keam critiques the national jingoism in much of the publicity for music emanating from New Zealand, linking it to the myths of "Kiwi" national identity which circulate in New Zealand of a "clean and green" country, down-to-earth, egalitarian and anti-intellectual in its orientation, ingenious (as in references to number eight wire being used to repair and construct almost everything), and jealously guarding its international achievements. There is little place in these myths for Māori notions of the

---

[13] Doreen Massey, *Space, Place, and Gender* (Minneapolis: University of Minnesota Press, 1994), 239.
[14] Ibid., 239–40.
[15] Glenda Keam, "Myths and Legends: Tales of Kiwi Musical Distinctiveness," in *Music on the Edge: Selected Papers from the 2007 IASPM Australia/New Zealand Conference*, ed. Dan Bendrups (Dunedin: International Association for the Study of Popular Music, Australia & New Zealand Chapter, 2008), 97.

land or identity, which film-maker Gaylene Preston articulates in Pākehā terms in relation to the extensive use of landscape in New Zealand cinema:

> Te whenua he whaea e kore e mate (The land is a mother that never dies). This Māori whatkatauaki (proverb) sums up an attitude many Māori and pākehā hold for the land. It is deeply embedded in our culture in a general sense and infuses New Zealand filmmaking with a spirit that permeates through the drama . . .
> There's a 'vibe'. You can feel it. Often dark, sometimes simple, I have never felt it anywhere else. It flows from the secrets the land holds. Tribal histories passed on by oral storytelling to the selected few; European settlers, recent arrivals without the language to express this place. Māori mythology as enduring as Homer is overlaid here with Celtic and European storytelling. . . . This expressive myth-making flows from the strength, the blood, the fire and the life of the land itself. Fresh ground for a new local artform.[16]

While many film critics have commented on the importance of landscape and place in New Zealand cinema by both Māori and Pākehā film makers,[17] there has been far less attention given to the importance of place and landscape in New Zealand music.[18]

## Music and Place in Aotearoa

As Keam has noted there is a long tradition of expressing the contours and resonances of landscape in the music of Aotearoa/New Zealand, as there is in its visual arts, dance, poetry, and literature.[19] This could be defined as a situated poetics, and related to *waiata* (song) and Māori creation myths, where the gods sang the world into existence, and the Sky Father (*Ranganui*) and Earth Mother (*Papatūānuku*) spawned other gods. Pre-European Māori sonic instruments, the *taonga puoro*, were largely

---

[16] Gaylene Preston, cited in Ian Brodie, *A Journey through New Zealand Film* (Auckland: HarperCollins, 2006), 8–9.

[17] Babington, *A History of the New Zealand Fiction Feature Film*; Martin Blythe, *Naming the Other: Images of the Māori in New Zealand Film and Television* (Metuchen, NJ: The Scarecrow Press, 1994); Erean Le Héron, "Placing Geographical Imagination in Film: New Zealand Filmmakers' Use of Landscape," *New Zealand Geographer* 60, no. 1 (2004): 60–66.

[18] Keam being a notable exception: Glenda Keam, "Exploring Notions of National Style: New Zealand Orchestral Music in the Late Twentieth Century" (Ph.D. diss., University of Auckland, 2006).

[19] Ibid.

built from artefacts taken from the land—shells, bones, flax, stone, *pounamu* (greenstone), wood, swamp reeds, snails, leaves, and feathers, among other materials.

Hirini Melbourne and Richard Nunns have demonstrated extensively the huge range of *taonga puoro*, as well as how sounds can be made directly from native flora and sound-making plants in Aotearoa.[20] Mervyn McLean has categorized pre-European Māori musical instruments into idiophones, or percussive instruments, such as the *pahu* (wooden gong), *tookere* (bone clappers), *pakuru* (mouth bow), and *rooria* (jew's harp); and aerophones such as the *purerehua* (bullroarer), *koororohuu* (whizzers), and numerous types of trumpets and flutes.[21] Many of these are now used in contemporary Māori music since their reconstruction has become increasingly widespread, following on from the work of Melbourne and Nunns. A relatively contemporary musical example, which demonstrates the relation of Māori music to land, is Hone Tuwhare's poem "Papa-tū-ā-nuku" (Earth Mother), which was set to music and sung by Hone Hurihanganui on the 2005 compilation *Tuwhare*:

> We are stroking, caressing the spine
> of the land.
> We are massaging the ricked
> back of the land
> with our sore but ever-loving feet:
> hell, she loves it!
> Squirming, the land wriggles
> in delight.
> We love her.[22]

Here the Earth Mother is personified as a lover responding physically and erotically to the caresses and footsteps of the people walking over her. The poem, one of many of Tuwhare's works set to music by New Zealand composers, also has a political dimension, being one of a number Tuwhare wrote commemorating the 1975 New Zealand Land March on Wellington, which covered 700 miles in 30 days and involved 40,000 people.[23] Such musical commemorations of land and place in Aotearoa/New Zealand exemplify explicitly the situatedness of so much music here, not in a

---

[20] See Mitchell, "The Sounds of Nowhere?" 222.

[21] Mervyn McLean, *Māori Music* (Auckland University Press, 1996), 166–200.

[22] Cited in Janet Hunt, *Hone Tuwhare: A Biography* (Auckland: Godwit, 1998), 131.

[23] Ibid., 131–35.

national context, but in terms of the importance of the particularities of where we come from and where we are, in the process of defining who we are.

# References

Babington, Bruce. *A History of the New Zealand Fiction Feature Film.* Manchester: Manchester University Press, 2007.
Blythe, Martin. *Naming the Other: Images of the Māori in New Zealand Film and Television.* Metuchen, NJ: The Scarecrow Press, 1994.
Brodie, Ian. *A Journey through New Zealand Film.* Auckland: HarperCollins, 2006.
Crowded House. *Together Alone.* Capitol Records 7243 8 27048 2 2, 1993.
*Don't Let It Get You.* Film. John O'Shea. Wellington: Pacific Films, 1966.
Flint, Michael. "What the Air Was Like Up There: Overseas Music and Local Reception in the 1960s." In *North Meets South: Popular Music in Aotearoa/New Zealand*, edited by Philip Hayward, Tony Mitchell, and Roy Shuker, 1–15. Sydney: Perfect Beat Publications, 1994.
Herriman, Nina. "The Air Down Here: Global and Local Interpretations of New Zealand Popular Music, 1955–1977." M.A. diss., University of Auckland, 2004.
Hunt, Janet. *Hone Tuwhare: A Biography.* Auckland: Godwit, 1998.
Keam, Glenda. "Exploring Notions of National Style: New Zealand Orchestral Music in the Late Twentieth Century." Ph.D. diss., University of Auckland, 2006.
—. "Myths and Legends: Tales of Kiwi Musical Distinctiveness." In *Music on the Edge: Selected Papers from the 2007 IASPM Australia/New Zealand Conference*, edited by Dan Bendrups, 68–74. Dunedin: IAPSM-ANZ, 2008.
Lealand, Geoff. *A Foreign Egg in Our Nest?* Wellington: Victoria University Press, 1988.
Le Héron, Erean. "Placing Geographical Imagination in Film: New Zealand Filmmakers' Use of Landscape." *New Zealand Geographer* 60, no. 1 (2004): 60–66.
Massey, Doreen. *Space, Place, and Gender.* Minneapolis: University of Minnesota Press, 1994.
McLean, Mervyn. *Māori Music.* Auckland: Auckland University Press, 1996.
Mitchell, Tony. "The Sounds of Nowhere? Bicultural Music in Aotearoa/New Zealand." In *Popular Music and Local Identity: Rock,*

*Pop and Rap in Europe and Oceania*, edited by Tony Mitchell, 215–62. London: Leicester University Press, 1996.

Russell, Bruce. "Biography," *NZ Electronic Poetry Centre Website*, http://www.nzepc.auckland.ac.nz.

Shuker, Roy, and Michael Pickering. "Kiwi Rock; Popular Music and Cultural Identity in New Zealand." *Popular Music* 13, no. 3 (1994): 261–78.

Street, John. "(Dis)located? Rhetoric, Politics, Meaning and the Locality." In *Popular Music: Style and Identity,* edited by Will Straw et al., 255–63. Montreal: Centre for Research on Canadian Cultural Industries and Institutions, 1995.

# CHAPTER THREE

# MIGRANT MUSIC IN NEW ZEALAND: ISSUES AND CONCEPTS

# DAN BENDRUPS

In a recent appraisal of Australian folk music history, musicologist Graeme Smith emphasized the importance of music as a representational medium for diverse communities, stating that music creates "images of past and present Australian experience and [projects] various versions of the relationship between individual experience, the community and the nation."[1] Like Australia, New Zealand is a nation founded on a series of migrations, and immigration continues to be a defining factor in the contemporary New Zealand cultural landscape. However, official discourses of New Zealand nationhood focus predominantly on the enduring modes of contact and engagement experienced and negotiated between Māori and Pākehā, to the exclusion of other culturally or ethnically-defined migrant groups. Consequently, while cultural diversity in New Zealand is celebrated, it is not integrated in a formal manner into the conceptualization of the nation, and cultural diversity remains an underexplored issue in relation to New Zealand identity.

The New Zealand government's policy of biculturalism is of vital importance to the construction of New Zealand identity as the primary vehicle for the reaffirmation of the indigenous culture of New Zealand, which had previously endured decades of official denigration and denial. Therefore, it is not surprising that a multicultural policy has not been adopted in New Zealand as it has been in comparative nations including Canada and Australia.[2] Biculturalism does not specifically contradict the

---

[1] Graeme Smith, *Singing Australian: A History of Folk and Country Music* (Melbourne: Pluto Press, 2005), x.
[2] Christine Cheyne, Mike O'Brien, and Michael Belgrave, *Social Policy in Aotearoa/New Zealand: A Critical Introduction* (Auckland: Oxford University Press, 2004).

multiculturalism of contemporary New Zealand society, but neither does it serve multiculturalism at an official level. Since the advent of new legal status being ascribed to the Treaty of Waitangi in 1975, "government-owned agencies . . . have been increasingly required to be bicultural—that is, to fairly represent Māori and non-Māori interests in their operations and their allocation of resources."[3] However, the reduction of all non-Māori New Zealanders to a single category marginalizes the representation of the many cultural and ethnic groups that are neither Māori nor Pākehā (who comprise the majority of the non-Māori population). In light of this enduring dichotomy, music (amongst other forms of cultural expression) provides non-Māori and non-Pākehā New Zealanders with a valuable mechanism for cultural representation.

This paper proposes a framework for the consideration of music as a marker of migrant cultural identity in New Zealand, which reflects the ways in which the experience of migration has affected subsequent musical participation by migrants. This paper proposes that migrant music performance in New Zealand can be divided into two categories: performance for the purpose of group commemoration; and performance for cultural, artistic, or personal expression. In general, migration patterns tend to lead performers in one of either of these two directions, though they are not mutually exclusive. This paper presents for discussion a variety of short case-study examples of migrant musics in New Zealand in order to demonstrate a broad, culturally- and ethnically-decentred approach to the topic. These examples all reflect very different migration conditions and circumstances; what they have in common is that they are drawn from current research being undertaken at the University of Otago by Henry Johnson and myself.

## Migration in Ethnomusicology

Migration is a topic of particular interest to the field of ethnomusicology. While early European and American ethnomusicologists were primarily concerned with the music of exotic and indigenous cultures, the urban turn of anthropology in the 1970s influenced a body of

---

[3] New Zealand Government Ministry for Culture and Heritage, "Cultural Policy in New Zealand," *Ministry for Culture and Heritage*, 2007, http://www.cultureandheritage.govt.nz/publications/cultural-policies/index.html#_Toc71523744.

research concerning "urban ethnomusicology"[4] that became a mainstay of the discipline in the late twentieth century. With the development of concepts such as insider- and auto-ethnography, and micro-music,[5] ethnomusicology changed from its original conceptualization as a field concerned with the music of "others" into a discipline capable of illuminating all musics through ethnographic research. This paradigm shift has facilitated the alignment of ethnomusicology and popular music studies in the last decade, as these two areas increasingly overlap in their relevance to the understanding of the global post-modern condition. It has also informed the way in which ethnomusicological frameworks have been applied to understanding the music cultures of immigrants in developed countries and metropolitan contexts.

Migrant music is of interest to ethnomusicology in two distinct ways: firstly, as the musical expression of migrants in host countries; and secondly, as the decontextualized reproduction of that music more widely within the host society, irrespective of the actual participation of migrant performers. Sometimes, a particular music culture may simultaneously occupy both fields of inquiry, as exemplified by Latin American-derived genres such as salsa. In New Zealand, salsa exists as a culturally decontextualized component of ballroom dancing, as a musical genre performed in jazz contexts, as the basis of a burgeoning recreational dance industry, and as a perceived "authentic" mode of expression of small communities of Latino/a migrants. While these contexts occasionally overlap in public events, such as cultural festivals, they essentially cater to distinct audiences within New Zealand society.

In Anglophone countries that have adopted multicultural policies, ethnomusicological research into migrant music has a rich history. In the United States, for example, migrant music has provided insight into the lives of urban migrant communities,[6] served to demonstrate the complex

---

[4] Peter Manuel, "New Perspectives in American Ethnomusicology," *TRANS—Transcultural Music Review* 1 (1995), http://www.sibetrans.com/trans/trans1/manuel.htm.

[5] See especially Gregory Barz and Timothy J. Cooley, eds., *Shadows in the Field: New Perspectives for Fieldwork in Ethnomusicology*, 2nd ed. (New York: Oxford, 2008); Mark Slobin, *Subcultural Sounds: Micromusics of the West* (Hanover: Wesleyan, 1993); Martin Stokes, ed., *Ethnicity and Identity in Music: The Musical Construction of Place* (Oxford: Berg, 1994).

[6] Adelaida Reyes-Schramm, "Explorations in Urban Ethnomusicology: Hard Lessons from the Spectacularly Ordinary," *Yearbook for Traditional Music* 14 (1982): 1–14.

position of Latin American identity within the United States,[7] provided an avenue for historical research into early European settlement and cultural legacy,[8] and provided a way of understanding the cultural outcomes of multiculturalism.[9]

Locally, migrant music has been a dominant aspect of Australian ethnomusicology for two generations of scholars, many of whom have been involved with migrant musics as performers or are themselves the descendents of non-Anglophone migrants to Australia. Examples include Margaret Kartomi's Jewish music research, Cathy Falk's research with the Hmong community, Helen O'Shea and Irish traditions, Mike Ryan's work with Brazilian migrants, Aline Scott-Maxwell's prolific engagement with Italian and Indonesian musicians, John Whiteoak's investigation of continental European ethnicities as a feature of historical popular music, and my own work with Latin American migrant musicians.[10]

In New Zealand, important research has been conducted into the music of specific European and Asian migrant groups,[11] but, separately to this, music provides the basis for a range of studies dealing with Pacific Islanders in the New Zealand context.[12] The bulk of this work has been undertaken outside a migration studies framework, using instead the discourses of media and popular culture to situate the contribution of Pasifika musicians to New Zealand music. A characteristic of the contextualization of Pacific Islanders in popular music discourse is that they inevitably get categorized according to genre, and therefore cohabit

---

[7] Frances Aparicio and Cándida Frances Jáquez, eds., *Musical Migrations: Transnationalism and Cultural Hybridity in Latin/o America* (New York: Palgrave Macmillan, 2003).

[8] Charles Keil and Angeliki Vellou Keil, *Polka Happiness* (Philadelphia: Temple University Press, 1992).

[9] Kip Lornell and Anne K. Rasmussen, eds., *Music of Multicultural America: A Study of Twelve Musical Communities* (New York: Schirmer Books, 1997).

[10] A number of these authors recently collaborated on a special issue of the *Victorian Historical Journal* devoted to "Music, Migration and Multiculturalism" (78, no. 2 (2007)).

[11] Dan Bendrups, "A Cultural History of the Christchurch Latvian Choir," in *Music on the Edge: Select Proceedings of the 2007 IASPM-ANZ Conference*, ed. Dan Bendrups (Dunedin: IAPSM-ANZ, 2008), 9–14; Henry Johnson, "'Happy Diwali!': Performance, Multicultural Soundscapes and Intervention in Aotearoa/New Zealand," *Ethnomusicology Forum* 16, no. 1 (2007): 71–94.

[12] Sarina Pearson, "Pasifik/NZ Frontiers: New Zealand-Samoan Hip Hop, Music Video, and Diasporic Space," *Perfect Beat* 6, no. 4 (2004): 55–66; Kirsten Zemke-White, "This is My Life: Biography, Identity and Narrative in New Zealand Rap Songs," *Perfect Beat* 8, no. 3 (2007): 31–51.

with Māori and Pākehā musicians with whom they may share certain expressive traits. This is demonstrated in Gareth Shute's populist book on hip hop in New Zealand, where little distinction is drawn between Māori and Pasifika performers, who are instead cast as having a shared musical heritage.[13] Such writing glosses over the systemic challenges faced by particular migrant groups and reaffirms the mainstream perception of New Zealand as a place that is sympathetic to cultural diversity, without subjecting this perception to critical analysis.

Similarly, the conceptualization of Pākehā identity suffers from overriding social generalizations. However, the musical life of Pākehā New Zealand reveals a plurality belied by the narrow contemporary application of the term. Nowhere is this more apparent than in the proliferation of highland bagpipe culture throughout New Zealand. The highland bagpipes serve a function in state-sanctioned ceremony— whether military or civilian—that is unconnected to the construction of Scottishness, but this limited public role is eclipsed in New Zealand by the sheer number of pipers and pipe bands throughout the country, some of whom have received international accolades. The dissemination of highland bagpipes in New Zealand is a reflection of a specific migration pattern encapsulated within the broader scope of nineteenth-century of pipe bands provides a unique perspective on where, when and how the Scottish diaspora became integrated into the nation. Many of these bands still exist, and they are testament to the symbolic and representational power of music in articulating cultural diversity and pluralism.

## Music as Commemorative Identity

The maintenance of highland piping traditions, particularly the highly specialized *piobaireachd*, is an example of the use of music for commemorative purposes by a migrant community. Commemoration, in this context, refers to the act of preservation where repertoire representative of an idealized collective identity is selected for performance—to the exclusion of individualistic compositions, avant garde repertoire, or other types of contemporary musical innovation. Commemoration is usually pursued by migrant groups who know or suspect that their migration is irrevocable and permanent. This was the case for many European settler groups who populated New Zealand in the nineteenth century, as it was also for post-war refugees in the mid-twentieth century. It also applies to the experience of asylum seekers

---

[13] Gareth Shute, *Hip Hop Music in Aotearoa* (Auckland: Reed, 2004).

fleeing more recent conflicts in Latin America, South-East Asia, and the Middle East.

Characteristically, music used for commemorative identity purposes is intended for performance and consumption within a closed group of community insiders. It maintains language and performance characteristics from the homeland unaltered, and the repertoire choices often reflect homeland songs and styles that were popular at the time of migration or which articulate something specific about homeland identity. In many cases, these songs continue to be performed without significant change over many decades, even if they change or become obsolete in the homeland itself. This music enacts a "museumification" of identity—a way of preserving the self in the face of unknown or unknowable cultural influences in the host country.

While commemorative preservation of music is often a deliberate choice, sometimes it is also a consequence of social and political circumstances beyond the control of culture bearers. For example, the Latvian community of New Zealand, based mainly in Christchurch, arrived as displaced persons in the aftermath of World War II because they were unable to return to Soviet-occupied Latvia for fear of persecution. This community was, essentially, cut off from their homeland, not only by the tyranny of distance, but also by an autocratic regime that imposed strict controls on communication, cultural production, and even language use for half a century. After three or four decades in exile, as the Soviet regime endured, many Latvians accepted that they would never be able to return home again. This did not, however, result in the abandonment of cultural practices significant to their pre-migratory lives, but quite the opposite. Songs remembered from the 1930s and '40s are still performed by Latvian musicians in New Zealand today, and some of these are no longer performed regularly in Latvia itself. Furthermore, Latvian musicians began to reflect on their situation in post-war New Zealand through the medium of song, employing the language and musical style of their homeland.

Since the return to democracy in Latvia in 1992, a trickle of new migrants have joined the Christchurch community, yet their acceptance is not guaranteed, and they need to endure a period of adjustment as they realize that their fellow community members represent a cultural derivation more than fifty years old. As one recent migrant in her early twenties told me, there are Latvians in Christchurch who she regards as being more fluent in Latvian language and culture than she is herself, even though they have been out of Latvia since before her own parents were born.

## Music as Expressive Identity

Converse to the use of music for commemoration is the use of music by migrants for aesthetic or cultural expression. This usage is most common amongst recent migrant groups, within communities that experience ongoing cross-migration to and from their homelands, and amongst temporary migrants who know or suspect that their stay in New Zealand is of limited duration. Some of these migrants are coincidental travelers to New Zealand, others migrate for work opportunities or because particular government policies or other enterprises facilitate their arrival and accommodation. Sometimes, as in the Latvian example, new migrants join older, established communities. Elsewhere, musical participation is strongest amongst new and emerging migrant communities not previously represented in New Zealand.

Characteristically, the use of music for expressive identity purposes draws on contemporary popular music repertoires. Rather than commemorating homeland identity, songs are chosen to articulate difference or create interest amongst a diverse audience. Lacking an established community, these musicians are adept at performing to and/or with cultural outsiders. Indeed, in some instances, such as the *taiko* drumming in the Waikato, which has been investigated by Henry Johnson, performances might involve a majority of cultural outsiders.[14]

Another prominent aspect of music as expressive identity is the construction, importation, and widespread use of iconic exotic instruments (often percussion) and other materials used in performance. This includes props, such as the performing lions and dragons used in Chinese rituals, which have only recently entered widespread public use despite many generations of Chinese settlement in New Zealand. Global markets and communication technology make it easier for recent migrants to access material goods from home, whereas previous waves of migrants lacked these markets, lacked financial access to them, or faced politically-imposed restrictions.

New Zealand's rapidly growing Brazilian community presents various examples of music serving as a vector of expressive identity. The widespread migration of Brazilians to New Zealand has occurred only in the last decade as a result of an improving Brazilian economy that affords more people the luxury of travel, and a New Zealand policy of openness

---

[14] Henry Johnson, "Why *Taiko*? Understanding *Taiko* Performance at New Zealand's 1st *Taiko* Festival," *Sites: A Journal of Social Anthropology and Cultural Studies* 5, no. 2 (2008): 111–34.

towards Brazil, reflected in the establishment of working-holiday and student visas for Brazilians. The migrants within this community are often young and single, and they are not charged with the task of maintaining homeland identity by their peers. Conversely, the global popular culture presence of Brazil—in sport, music, and festivals—ensures that New Zealanders actively seek access to homeland performance practice from the new migrants, who are instead faced with a different dilemma. As one Queenstown-based singer told me, "Back home I sing rock. That's it. But here, when people find out I'm Brazilian and that I'm a singer, they all ask me to sing *bossa nova*." Public enthusiasm for Brazilian popular music has forced this singer to adopt aspects of Brazilian music that did not previously form part of her performance identity, but which are expected of her in the New Zealand context. In other words, the expression of migrant identity, in this case, is manifest as a matter of public interest.

## Conclusion

The pluralism and sheer cultural diversity of contemporary New Zealand society is a situation beyond the imagining of previous generations, and the engineers of current public policy are faced with significant challenges in seeking to accommodate the extent of cultural change that characterizes the twenty-first century nation. While it is not often that musicians have the power, individually or collectively, to influence public policy, this paper indicates that they do control a form of expression that has the capacity to transcend private and public space. Music therefore serves a vital social function in New Zealand as a vehicle for the expression of identity that is otherwise not afforded public acknowledgement. For this reason, the unique role of music in articulating many facets of New Zealand cultural identity deserves continued scholarly attention.

## References

Aparicio, Frances, and Cándida Frances Jáquez, eds. *Musical Migrations: Transnationalism and Cultural Hybridity in Latin/o America.* New York: Palgrave Macmillan, 2003.

Barz, Gregory, and Timothy J. Cooley, eds. *Shadows in the Field: New Perspectives for Fieldwork in Ethnomusicology,* 2nd ed. New York: Oxford, 2008.

Bendrups, Dan. "A Cultural History of the Christchurch Latvian Choir." In *Music on the Edge: Select Proceedings of the 2007 IASPM-ANZ*

*Conference*, edited by Dan Bendrups, 9–14. Dunedin: IAPSM-ANZ, 2008.

Cheyne, Christine, Mike O'Brien, and Michael Belgrave. *Social Policy in Aotearoa/New Zealand: A Critical Introduction*. Auckland: Oxford University Press, 2004.

Johnson, Henry. "'Happy Diwali!': Performance, Multicultural Soundscapes and Intervention in Aotearoa/New Zealand." *Ethnomusicology Forum* 16, no. 1 (2007): 71–94.

—. "Why *Taiko*? Understanding *Taiko* Performance at New Zealand's 1st *Taiko* Festival." *Sites: A Journal of Social Anthropology and Cultural Studies* 5, no. 2 (2008): 111–34.

Keil, Charles, and Angeliki Vellou Keil. *Polka Happiness*. Philadelphia: Temple University Press, 1992.

Lornell, Kip, and Anne K. Rasmussen, eds. *Music of Multicultural America: A Study of Twelve Musical Communities*. New York: Schirmer Books, 1997.

Manuel, Peter. "New Perspectives in American Ethnomusicology," *TRANS—Transcultural Music Review* 1 (1995), http://www.sibetrans.com/trans/trans1/manuel.htm.

New Zealand Government Ministry for Culture and Heritage, "Cultural Policy in New Zealand," *Ministry for Culture and Heritage*, 2007, http://www.cultureandheritage.govt.nz/publications/cultural-policies/index.html#_Toc71523744.

Pearson, Sarina. "Pasifik/NZ Frontiers: New Zealand-Samoan Hip Hop, Music Video, and Diasporic Space." *Perfect Beat* 6, no. 4 (2004): 55–66.

Reyes-Schramm, Adelaida. "Explorations in Urban Ethnomusicology: Hard Lessons from the Spectacularly Ordinary." *Yearbook for Traditional Music* 14 (1982): 1–14.

Shute, Gareth. *Hip Hop Music in Aotearoa*. Auckland: Reed, 2004.

Slobin, Mark. *Subcultural Sounds: Micromusics of the West*. Hanover: Wesleyan, 1993.

Smith, Graeme. *Singing Australian: A History of Folk and Country Music*. Melbourne: Pluto Press, 2005.

Stokes, Martin, ed. *Ethnicity and Identity in Music: The Musical Construction of Place*. Oxford: Berg, 1994.

*Victorian Historical Journal* 78, no. 2 (2007).

Zemke-White, Kirsten. "This is My Life: Biography, Identity and Narrative in New Zealand Rap Songs." *Perfect Beat* 8, no. 3 (2007): 31–51.

# CHAPTER FOUR

## SOUNDING OUT THE STREETS: PERFORMANCE, CULTURAL IDENTITY, AND PLACE IN WELLINGTON'S CUBA STREET CARNIVAL

## SHELLEY D. BRUNT

In early 2009, a new radio campaign was launched in Wellington. Using voices from a variety of local residents, the advertisements pitched ideas for music performances in the Cuba Street Carnival: a biennial, all-day, free festival staged in the inner city streets. These proposals—such as one to broadcast a jungle-gumbo/surf-core soundtrack with Scandinavian opera, and another to stage a Brazilian samba concert with dancers in carnival costumes—introduced two of the Carnival's key aims. Firstly, to be the largest showcase of diverse music from New Zealand and, secondly, to celebrate the music from Wellington's cultural groups.[1] It is these notions of place and cultural identity in Cuba Street Carnival performances that are explored in this paper, in order to "sound out" the music of Wellington in 2009.

This paper represents the first stage of new research on this iconic event on Wellington's local cultural calendar. It stems from fieldwork conducted at the February 21, 2009 event, where I attended performances and participated in the Illuminated Night Parade, and also draws from media reports and interview material. Due to the recent timing of the Carnival, I will use this forum to "sound out" my preliminary ideas, with a view to progressing the research. This paper adopts a visually- and textually-based framework and methodology, with a view to further developing a method of musical analysis to explore the dialogic processes

---

[1] Chris Morley-Hall, "The Parade Mission," *Parade Entry Kit 2009: Cuba Street Carnival* (Wellington: n.p., 2008), 2.

that exist between performer and listener. Beginning with an historical overview of the Carnival, this paper examines how a sense of place is constructed for Wellington's Cuba Street, before concluding with a discussion of cultural identity in relation to the Carnival.

## Carnival Overview

Although small, carnival-style events took place in Cuba Street throughout the 1990s, the first Cuba Street Carnival was staged in 1999 by the current artistic director, Chris Morley-Hall.[2] As an immigrant who had only moved to New Zealand from the UK one year prior, Morley-Hall's connection with the bohemian street was admittedly tenuous. Even so, his past involvement with multicultural events, such as the prestigious Notting Hill Street Carnival in London and his connections with the Rio de Janeiro Carnival, served to establish a benchmark for his vision of New Zealand's own Carnival. With the aim of celebrating "the distinctive artistic culture of Wellington's most loved street," the first Carnival was held over three days and attracted a sizable audience of 15,000 people who browsed market stalls and attended performances by (then) up-and-coming local bands such as Fat Freddy's Drop.[3] Morley-Hall has directed all of the Carnivals since then, including the 2009 event which was promoted as the 10th anniversary of the first Carnival. His aim for this landmark Carnival, as boldly stated on the official application form for participants, was to continue to be "the most extraordinary, diverse, creative and successful inner city celebration in New Zealand, transforming Wellington's streets into a free explosion of colour, sound and performance, which consumes, inspires, interacts and engages its audience."[4]

Music clearly lies at the heart of the Carnival. Throughout the event, bands and soloists were featured on ten individually-themed stages, including the Zeal Street Culture Stage ("a showcase of Wellington's hottest up-and-coming acts"), the Hope Bros Stage ("purveyors of the latest and greatest in NZ music"), and the Havana Club Square ("music, mojitos and all things Latin American").[5] In addition, there were non-musical activities and events (such as sideshow rides, food stalls, craft markets, outdoor pubs, and roaming visual artists), and the Carnival

---

[2] Chris Morley-Hall, interview by author, January 30, 2009.
[3] *The 10 Most Fabulous Features of the Cuba Street Carnival* (Wellington: n.p., 2009), 1.
[4] *Parade Entry Kit 2009: Cuba Street Carnival* (Wellington: n.p., 2008), 16.
[5] *Cuba Street Carnival Pocket Programme 2009* (Wellington: n.p., 2009), n.p.

concluded with the grand Illuminated Night Parade that traveled in procession through the streets after dark. Due to the multifaceted nature of the Carnival, and to accommodate the estimated crowd of 150,000 people, the Carnival now closes over one square kilometre of Wellington's streets, including Cuba Street itself (fig. 4-1).[6]

Moving beyond the structural organisation of—and vision for—the Carnival, this event is clearly presented as a public celebration of social and cultural unity. It also has implications for understanding the construction and negotiation of identity and place.[7]

## Constructing a Sense of Place:
## Cuba Street, Wellington

Cultural and artistic events play an increasingly significant role in creating distinct place-identities for cities and regions in New Zealand. A sense of place is constructed, enacted, and rhetorically defended with an eye (and ear) on others and other locations.[8] In the case of the Cuba Street Carnival, place is significant in the staging of the event and, in turn, the Carnival also plays a significant role in the construction of a distinct place in New Zealand. This place—Wellington, the capital of New Zealand and home to the seat of parliament—is a geographically compact city set on the edge of a harbour, with rolling hills providing a natural backdrop for the small skyscrapers. Often hailed as a vibrant and creative destination with a multicultural population unlike any other in the country, Wellington also hosts many festivals associated with these migrant communities, such as the Diwali Festival of Lights, Pasifika, and the Asian Night Market. These events have been incorporated into the official discourse surrounding the city, with the Wellington City Council branding Wellington New Zealand's "Culture Capital," "Creative Capital," and "Events Capital," to distinguish the city from other New Zealand destinations. The concept of cultural tourism is particularly relevant in this construction of place. Not only can the Cuba Street Carnival's "geographical theme and sloganeering" be considered part of the city's

---

[6] Tom Cardy, "Streets Ahead of Last Carnival," *The Dominion Post*, February 23, 2009.
[7] Martin Stokes, "Introduction: Ethnicity, Identity and Music," in *Ethnicity, Identity and Music: The Musical Construction of Place,* ed. Martin Stokes (Oxford: Berg, 1994), 3.
[8] Martin Stokes, "Music and the Global Order," *Annual Review of Anthropology* 33 (2004): 50.

construction of locality,[9] but it is through this event that we find "the commodification of local culture and heritage" of Wellington.[10] Moreover, if the essence of the Carnival is Cuba Street, as Morley-Hall has claimed, then it is important to briefly highlight the history and cultural significance of this area, which gives name to—and physically demarcates the spaces of—the Carnival.

Cuba Street was named after the early settler ship "Cuba" (which was, in turn, named after the island nation), and today the street and the shops in the surrounding area still uphold the Cuban connection. This is seen in business names such as Havana Coffee Works and Havana Club, which refer to the Cuban capital, as well as Fidel's Café and Ernesto's, which acknowledge Fidel Castro and Che Guevara as key figures in the Cuban Revolution. These references provide a theme for the district, but also aptly reflect the street's own history as a site for social change in Wellington. Most notable was the 1932 Cuba Street Riot following the Great Depression, when street residents were among the poorest in the city and the government failed to meet the people's needs for food and employment opportunities.[11] The street has also been associated with cultural diversity; from the migrant workers who manned the fish markets, to the entrepreneurial Greek immigrants who opened milk bars, and the Dutch who turned them into coffee houses, helping to shape Cuba Street's café scene.[12]

One of the major instigators in shaping Cuba Street's distinctive culture was the recently implemented inner-city bypass. A proposal for a traffic bypass that would affect the street had "sat on the drawing board since the late 1960s," so there had been little maintenance on many buildings because of the assumption that they were going to be torn down at some point.[13] As a result, a proliferation of second-hand and bargain shops emerged in the run-down buildings, which led to the birth of the street's reputation as Wellington's bohemian zone. This was reinforced in

---

[9] Sara Cohen, "Liverpool and the Beatles: Exploring Relations between Music and Place, Text and Context," in *Keeping Score: Music, Disciplinarity, Culture*, ed. David Schwarz, Anahid Kassabian, and Lawrence Siegel (Charlottesville: University of Virginia Press, 1997), 105.
[10] Cohen, "Liverpool and the Beatles," 91.
[11] Pat Lawlor, *Pat Lawlor's Wellington* (Wellington: Millwood Press, 1976), 153–62.
[12] Zisis Bruce Blades, *Wellington's Hellenic Mile: The Greek Shops of the Twentieth Century* (Wellington: Precise Print, 2005).
[13] "Cuba Street the Star of History Website," *The Dominion Post,* November 19, 2008, http://www.stuff.co.nz/dominion-post/news/wellington/726128.

1969 when part of the street was permanently blocked off from traffic to
create Cuba Mall, which became home to shops and trendy eateries and
bars. In recent years, the implementation of the city bypass has meant that
Cuba Street has been cut in half, forcing Carnival organisers to expand the
event into neighbouring streets for logistical reasons. Today, the street
encompasses all of these mixed elements. It is, in equal parts, pedestrian
mall and road, and it houses an eclectic mix of sex shops, tattooists, bars,
music retailers, coffee shops, textile stores, independent ateliers, and
community venues.

An examination of the social and cultural meanings produced in a
music event such as the Cuba Street Carnival inevitably involves an
examination of the locations in which music is performed. Urban spaces
provide "the socio-cultural backdrop for distinctive musical practices and
innovations," and also the "rich experiential settings in which music is
consumed."[14] Music can also be a key resource for cultural groups to make
sense of, and negotiate, everyday spaces.[15] While the biennial Carnival is
not an "everyday" activity, its location in the heart of "Creative
Wellington" and its transformation of urban city streets to a zone of
music-making and social revelry can be considered a site for the
presentation of distinctive musical practices of cultural groups. This site
and the identities associated with it are not fixed but fluid, and can be
described as a natural "landscape of tourists, immigrants, exiles and other
moving groups and persons."[16] At this point, I would like to consider how
the identities and the "many voices" of Wellington's diverse communities
are represented in the landscape of the Carnival, by examining two events:
the Illuminated Night Parade and the Asia Bazaar.

## "Many Voices": The Illuminated Night Parade
## and the Asia Bazaar

At 9 p.m. when the sun had set, the first of the thirty-six floats and
walking groups of the Illuminated Night Parade rolled down the nightlife
strip of Courtenay Place and past the crowds of people wedged against

---

[14] Andy Bennett, "Introduction: Part 1: Music, Space and Place," in *Music, Space
and Place: Popular Music and Cultural Identity*, ed. Sheila Whiteley, Andy
Bennett, and Stan Hawkins (Burlington: Ashgate, 2004), 2.

[15] Tia DeNora, *Music in Everyday Life* (New York: Cambridge, 2000).

[16] Arjun Appadurai, "Global Ethnoscapes: Notes and Queries for a Transnational
Anthropology," in *Recapturing Anthropology: Working in the Present*, ed. Richard
G. Fox (Sante Fe: SAR Press, 1991), 192.

street barriers. Like a compilation CD of world music which shifts from aural representations of one country to the next—mirroring the global flows of music—the motion of the parade past the stationary listener meant that new music faded in and out with the passing of each float. The unfolding of a performance such as this plays a significant role in the creation of meaning.[17] Indeed, upon first consideration, the parade highlights a diverse soundscape of musical and cultural identities in New Zealand, with performances from Caribbean steel drummers, Scottish pipers (fig. 4-2), Cook Island log drummers, Japanese *taiko* players, and Brazillian *batucada* perfomers, among others.

The Parade is an overt celebration of multiculturalism in a city where, only a few blocks away, the formal discourse of biculturalism is officially sanctioned and enforced in The Beehive (New Zealand's parliament). But the Parade also facilitates a form of what Johnson called "ethnic tourism" in his writing on Indonesian *gamelan* in New Zealand.[18] In the context of the Carnival, listeners "consume the sounds of exotic others as outsiders, without understanding musical or cultural contexts" for there is little signage, or indeed explanation from Carnival staff by way of programme, as to who is performing on these floats.[19] Are the steel drum percussionists members of Wellington's Caribbean community, or are they present to publicise the new Calypso Caribbean restaurant off Cuba Street? The categories of "community," "small business," and "corporate" which are delineated in the Parade application form are blurred in the actual performances.

In contrast with the Night Parade is the Asia Bazaar: a new addition to the 2009 Carnival that is funded through the Asia:New Zealand Foundation. Featuring an all-day marketplace and food stalls hosted by local Asian restaurants, the focal point of the Bazaar is a small, elevated stage on Dixon Street, off Cuba Mall. Here, a range of "Asian" performances are on display, from an Indian woman singing Bollywood hits to a backing CD, to a Korean ensemble performing *samulnori* (traditional percussion) (fig. 4-3).

Unlike the Illuminated Night Parade, which was moderated by a board of trustees and for which entrance was open to all Wellingtonians who

---

[17] See Nicholas Cook and Mark Everest, eds., *Rethinking Music* (Oxford: Oxford University Press, 1999).
[18] Henry Johnson, "Striking Accord! Gamelan, Education, and Indonesian Cultural Flows in Aotearoa/New Zealand," in *Asia in the Making of New Zealand*, ed. Henry Johnson and Brian Moloughney (Auckland: Auckland University Press, 2006), 191.
[19] Ibid., 191.

applied for a float permit, the Asia Bazaar was solely curated by Murali
Kumar, a member of Wellington's Indian community who had no real ties
to the core Carnival team. During one recent interview, he stated that he
had his own visions for the Bazaar and its music performance. These were
"promoting the culture; retaining the culture; [and] sharing the culture
with others."[20] What was meant by "the culture" as a singular entity, or
even the more implicitly plural "Asian cultures" in the context of the
Bazaar is arguable, but the role of music "as a device for building unity
between and across immigrant communities" is patent.[21] Moreover, the
presence of multicultural music also helps to "create culture and cultural
understanding" and aids in the negotiation of the kind of "transcultural
sense of place" that is Wellington.[22] Music in the context of the Asia
Bazaar no doubt serves as "an emblem of cultural identity, whether
transmitted, modified, or invented."[23] As observed by one audience
member, second generation Chinese New Zealander Linda Lims, the
musical performances in the Asia Bazaar served as a visible form of
cultural recognition of her community by others, and vice versa:

> It is nice to see the Asian community, who have been such an important
> part of Wellington for so long, . . . actually embrace the Cuba Street
> Carnival and become an integral part of it. I guess it sort of shows that [we
> have] truly come of age, and really [have] been accepted as part of
> Wellington's community, to finally be involved in such an iconic event for
> the city.[24]

Following Martin Stokes' writing about Turkish and Irish immigrants,
musical events can evoke and organize the "collective memories" for
migrants and "present experiences of place with an intensity, power and
simplicity unmatched by any other social activity."[25] But is the Asia
Bazaar an example of "music as commemoration" or "music as cultural
expression," as delineated by Dan Bendrups in this volume? This remains
to be seen. What is evident, however, is that the musical performances
from Wellington's Asian diaspora are framed according to an outsider's

---

[20] Kumar, cited in Bharat Jamnadas, "Street Full of Fun," *Asia Downunder*, TV
One television programme. Broadcast March 15, 2009.
[21] George Lipsitz, *Dangerous Crossroads: Popular Music, Postmodernism and the
Poetics of Place* (London: Verso, 1994), 126.
[22] Johnson, "Striking Accord!" 187.
[23] Ibid., 188.
[24] Bharat Jamnadas, "Street Full of Fun."
[25] Stokes, "Introduction: Ethnicity, Identity and Music," 3.

perspective, in spite of the curator's own connections with the Asian community. For example, the official programme announced a music programme featuring the "Colours of Vietnam," "Indian Delights," "Glorious Thai," and the "Beautiful Philippines"—perhaps not dissimilar to a travel brochure or dinner menu at an Asian restaurant, in that there was "something for everyone." It is this kind of discourse that exoticizes cultural groups and strips them of the specifics of their cultures.

## Conclusion

The examples presented here indicate that cultural tourism in Wellington, as in many other places, is as much about educating locals as it is about entertaining outsiders. Bound up in this idea is the notion that music can be used to express one's cultural and ethnic origins. Music also underscores and transforms individual and collective identity for Wellington's residents, and this is played out within the discourse of cultural plurality within contemporary New Zealand. Furthermore, "music is deeply implicated in the construction of place, and individual and group identities are tied into this construction."[26] For performers and participants alike, Wellington's Cuba Street Carnival can be a means of "sounding out the streets,"[27] that is, to audibly showcase New Zealand's music in the urban spaces of the nation's capital, and to negotiate cultural identity and a sense of place.

## References

Appadurai, Arjun. "Global Ethnoscapes: Notes and Queries for a Transnational Anthropology." In *Recapturing Anthropology: Working in the Present*, edited by Richard G. Fox, 191–210. Sante Fe: SAR Press, 1991.
Bennett, Andy. "Introduction: Part 1: Music, Space and Place." In *Music, Space and Place: Popular Music and Cultural Identity*, edited by Sheila Whiteley, Andy Bennett, and Stan Hawkins, 2–7. Burlington: Ashgate, 2004.

---

[26] Keith Kahn-Harris, "'Roots'?: The Relationship Between the Global and the Local within the Extreme Metal Scene," in *The Popular Music Studies Reader*, ed. Andy Bennett, Barry Shank, and Jason Toynbee (London: Routledge, 2005), 133.
[27] Cf. Sara Cohen, "Sounding out the City: Music and the Sensuous Production of Place," in *The Place of Music*, ed. Andrew Leyshon, David Matless, and George Revill (London: The Guildford Press, 1998), 286–87.

Blades, Zisis Bruce. *Wellington's Hellenic Mile: The Greek Shops of the Twentieth Century*. Wellington: Precise Print, 2005.

Cardy, Tom. "Streets Ahead of Last Carnival." *The Dominion Post*, February 23, 2009.

Cohen, Sara. "Liverpool and the Beatles: Exploring Relations Between Music and Place, Text and Context." In *Keeping Score: Music, Disciplinarity, Culture*, edited by David Schwarz, Anahid Kassabian, and Lawrence Siegel, 90–106. Charlottesville: University of Virginia Press, 1997.

—. "Sounding out the City: Music and the Sensuous Production of Place." In *The Place of Music*, edited by Andrew Leyshon, David Matless, and George Revill, 269–90. London: Guildford Press, 1998.

Cook, Nicholas, and Mark Everest, eds. *Rethinking Music*. Oxford: Oxford University Press, 1999.

*Cuba Street Carnival Pocket Programme 2009*. Wellington: n.p., 2009.

"Cuba Street the Star of History Website." *The Dominion Post,* November 19, 2008, http://www.stuff.co.nz/dominion-post/news/wellington/726128.

DeNora, Tia. *Music in Everyday Life*. New York: Cambridge, 2000.

Jamnadas, Bharat. "Street Full of Fun." *Asia Downunder*. Television Show. Auckland: TV One, 2009.

Johnson, Henry. "Striking Accord! Gamelan, Education, and Indonesian Cultural Flows in Aotearoa/New Zealand." In *Asia in the Making of New Zealand*, edited by Henry Johnson and Brian Moloughney, 185–203. Auckland: Auckland University Press, 2006.

Kahn-Harris, Keith. "'Roots'? The Relationship Between the Global and the Local within the Extreme Metal Scene." In *The Popular Music Studies Reader*, edited by Andy Bennett, Barry Shank, and Jason Toynbee, 128–34. London: Routledge, 2005.

Lawlor, Pat. *Pat Lawlor's Wellington*. Wellington: Millwood Press, 1976.

Lipsitz, George. *Dangerous Crossroads: Popular Music, Postmodernism and the Poetics of Place*. London: Verso, 1994.

Morley-Hall, Chris. "The Parade Mission." *Parade Entry Kit 2009: Cuba Street Carnival*. Wellington: n.p., 2008.

*Parade Entry Kit 2009: Cuba Street Carnival*. Wellington: n.p., 2008.

Stokes, Martin. "Introduction: Ethnicity, Identity and Music." In *Ethnicity, Identity and Music: The Musical Construction of Place,* edited by Martin Stokes, 1–28. Oxford: Berg, 1994.

—. "Music and the Global Order." *Annual Review of Anthropology* 33 (2004): 47–72.

*The 10 Most Fabulous Features of the Cuba Street Carnival*. Wellington: n.p., 2009.

Figure. 4-1. View along Cuba Street, Cuba Street Carnival 2009.    Source:
photographed by author.

Figure 4-2. Piping Band at the Illuminated Night Parade, Cuba Street Carnival
2009. Source: photographed by author.

Figure 4-3. Korean Percussion at the Asia Bazaar, Cuba Street Carnival 2009. Source: photographed by author.

# CHAPTER FIVE

## DRUMMING UP JAPAN:
## WHAT DOES IT MEAN TO BE A *TAIKO*
## PLAYER IN NEW ZEALAND?

## HENRY JOHNSON

*Taiko* performance is particularly visible and audible with its characteristic choreographed body movements, loud percussive music, and eye-catching drums. New Zealand has a small number of amateur Japanese *taiko* drum groups that have been established over the last two decades. Each of these groups shares the common goal of replicating Japanese-style drumming, and actively borrows and learns from established and more recent players in New Zealand, as well as from short-term visiting Japanese drummers. Such is the interest in *taiko* that in 2008 New Zealand held its first Taiko Festival, which attracted six of the nine committed New Zealand groups; approximately forty players.[1]

---

[1] On *taiko* playing within and outside Japan see further, for example, Jane Alaszewska, "Kumi-daiko," in *Grove Music Online. Oxford Music Online*, 2008, http://www.oxfordmusiconline.com/subscriber/article/grove/music/49402; Hugh de Ferranti, "Japan Beating: The Making and Marketing of Professional Taiko Music in Australia," in *Popular Culture, Globalization and Japan*, ed. Matthew Allen and Rumi Sakamoto (New York: Routledge, 2006); Linda Fujie, "Japanese Taiko Drumming in International Performance: Converging Musical Ideas in the Search for Success on Stage," *The World of Music* 43, nos. 2–3 (2001): 93–101; Sarah Hennessy, "'Taiko SouthWest': Developing a 'New' Musical Tradition in English Schools," *International Journal of Music Education* 23, no. 3 (2005): 217–25; Izumi Masumi, "Reconsidering Ethnic Culture and Community: A Case Study on Japanese Canadian Taiko Drumming," *Journal of Asian American Studies* 4, no. 1 (2001): 35–56; Henry Johnson, "Why *Taiko*? Understanding *Taiko* Performance at New Zealand's 1st *Taiko* Festival," *Sites: A Journal of Social Anthropology and Cultural Studies* 5, no. 2 (2008): 111–34; Henry Johnson, "Musical Moves and Transnational Grooves: Education, Transplantation and

This paper examines what it means to be a *taiko* player in New Zealand. The aim of the discussion is to uncover tropes of meaning pertaining to what it means to play instruments and music which have either been transplanted from one side of the Pacific to another or, in some way, maintain Japanese connections or associations. This paper is based on ethnographic research with several of the main groups and key individuals, as well as attendance at the 2008 Taiko Festival and other performances. It shows that, while players have some individual ideas on why they participate in this style of drumming, there are several underpinning concepts that help indicate what it means to be a *taiko* player in New Zealand. I will focus on several of these, especially one that was identified and offered in connection with the idea of cultural exchange. The paper will ultimately shed light on processes in New Zealand with regard to social and cultural influences, something that will act as an historical marker in understanding not only one transplanted musical form, but also some modern-day meanings concerning ethnicity, culture, and identity in New Zealand.

With such a research question, there are inherent assumptions, challenges and obstacles which need to be addressed. There is a sociological quandary, a "predicament of culture."[2] As well as attempting to understand meaning for selected individuals within the geographically- and nationally-bound context of New Zealand, which is an onerous yet fascinating task for any social scientist, there are also questions that need to be asked with regard to notions—essentialist or otherwise—of whether groups of *taiko* players form a social or cultural category for study in the first place. Do *taiko* players in New Zealand share a culture? Do they share an identity? Do they share an ethnicity?

A comparison to a point offered by anthropologist James Clifford about the Native American Mashpee provides a constructive perspective

Japanese *Taiko* Drumming at The International Pacific College, New Zealand," in *Recentring Asia: Histories, Encounters, Identities*, ed. Jacob Edmond, Henry Johnson, and Jacqueline Leckie (Folkestone: Global Oriental, in press); Deborah A. Wong, *Speak it Louder: Asian Americans Making Music* (New York: Routledge, 2004); Wong, "Noisy Intersection: Ethnicity, Authenticity and Ownership in Asian American Taiko," in *Diasporas and Interculturalism in Asian Performing Arts: Translating Traditions*, ed. Hae-kyung Um (New York: RoutledgeCurzon, 2005); Paul Jong Chul Yoon, "'She's Really Become Japanese Now!': Taiko Drumming and Asian American Identifications," *American Music* 19, no. 4 (2001): 417–38.

[2] James Clifford, *The Predicament of Culture: Twentieth-Century Ethnography, Literature, and Art* (Cambridge, Mass.: Harvard University Press, 1988).

on some of these issues.[3] Clifford's example was in connection with a court hearing over a piece of land. In summary, around three hundred Mashpee were required to show that they embodied a single tribe, a single culture with which each identified. In the end, the Mashpee lost their case because the jury could not define a set of Mashpee cultural characteristics. In connection with the dispute and Clifford's exposition of it, Japanologist Tessa Morris-Suzuki comments that "it is possible for a large number of people to identify themselves as 'Japanese' without sharing a single discernable 'culture' in the sense of agreeing *what it is that makes them 'Japanese.'*"[4] In other words, "it is not necessary for people who share a common 'identity' to share a common 'culture.'"[5] For example, an individual may identify with Japan as the place of his/her national identity, but not have cultural traits that are distinctly similar to some other Japanese.

The case in point is made more complex in connection with diaspora studies, whether long-term generational migration or medium- or short-term relocation. Moreover, when one overlaps diaspora studies with other cultural and global flows, the idea of identifying with one or more cultures fundamentally challenges the notion of national identity, indexing transnationalism and transculturalism.

For the purposes of this study, the New Zealand context is defined physically: *taiko* players are physically located within a geographically-bound nation-state; but the very existence in New Zealand of these instruments, the music, and the players raises further questions about place and culture. While *taiko* has a cultural "home" in Japan, does one have to be Japanese to be a *taiko* player? To turn Morris-Suzuki's conundrum around, it is not necessary for people who share a common "culture" (or part of one) to share a common "identity." Put another way, while one does not have to be Japanese or be in Japan to play *taiko*, when practising this Japanese performing art is one being or becoming Japanese? It is from this perspective that this discussion examines the place and meaning of *taiko* performance in New Zealand.

---

[3] Ibid.
[4] Tessa Morris-Suzuki, *Re-inventing Japan: Time, Space, Nation* (Armonk: M.E. Sharpe, 1998), 208.
[5] Ibid., 207.

# Ethnicity, Identity, and Culture

For any cultural theorist, ethnicity, identity, and culture are powerful terms that are loaded with meaning and often highly contentious. They resonate with critical discussion and demand clarification. However, rather than dwelling too much on definitions, classifications, and cultural theory, for the purpose of this brief synopsis I intend to use such terms as conduits for raising questions about the place of *taiko* in New Zealand, and for challenging notions of identity.

That my field research was undertaken in New Zealand points initially to a nationally-bound context. Yet, when the research is about drums that maintain a sense of having a cultural home in Japan, even if they were actually made in North America or in New Zealand, ideas of nationhood or national identity begin to break down, or at least are questioned.

New Zealand today is a distinctly multicultural nation within a bicultural political milieu. It has a history of migrations, some centuries old and others more recent. In this context, the place of *taiko* drumming in New Zealand is hardly controversial or surprising, particularly when one considers the global influences on the setting: for example, *gamelan*, *samba*, *capoeira*, and reggae groups; players of *sitar*, *tabla*, *koto*, and *shakuhachi*; and a consumer-oriented society that celebrates the planet's musical diversity by purchasing music (whether albums or downloads) or paying to attend live music performances.

The ethnicity of *taiko* players in New Zealand has had a profound influence on the groups. While Japanese players feature in some of the groups, and several groups are made up either entirely or almost entirely of Japanese, questions are raised regarding player identity. What does it mean to be a Japanese *taiko* player in New Zealand? What does it mean to be a non-Japanese *taiko* player in New Zealand?

One group that is made up mainly of Japanese is considered further on, but for now I will focus on some of the other groups. To be a Japanese *taiko* player in New Zealand brings with it a sense of authenticity. That is, authenticity for players who look the part and who have the cultural roots of *taiko* performance, regardless of how good the players actually are, or of their cultural knowledge. For instance, some non-Japanese players mentioned during field research that they found it very interesting when audiences were obviously extremely surprised to find out that the *taiko* players were not actually Japanese.

Performing, playing, and learning *taiko* has enormous meaning for many *taiko*-ists in New Zealand. Regardless of their ethnicity, their participation in rehearsals and performances seems to give players an immense sense of cultural or musical identity. For these players, being a *taiko* player is part of their cultural identity; it is part of who they are, where they are at, and where they are going.

While some players from the short-term diaspora (e.g., international tertiary students or short-term migrant workers) develop and consolidate their Japanese cultural identity as a result of being Japanese in New Zealand, many other players are not Japanese, yet embrace what is viewed as Japanese culture in similarly profound ways, and use this culture to express their own identity.

*Taiko* players in New Zealand share a culture: *taiko* playing. They may not share an ethnicity, but the *taiko* aspect which they embrace helps construct their identity in the New Zealand context. To put it another way, these *taiko* players identify with the culture of *taiko* performance, regardless of their ethnicity or identity.

## Tropes of Drumming

The tropes of drumming that were identified, either through self-identification or through ethnographic observation, have much to do with ethnicity, identity, and culture. The notion of culture exchange was offered by several of the players in Kodama, a group based at the International Pacific College (hereafter IPC) in Palmerston North (fig. 5-1). As well as the College itself including this way of thinking, the students themselves promote this idea in their own ways.

The *taiko* group at IPC is one based primarily on Japanese ethnicity. Most of the players, who vary from year to year as students enter and graduate from this tertiary institution, are Japanese. While several non-Japanese players currently and previously have played in the group, Japanese students dominate for two main reasons: the first is that IPC was founded by a Japanese organization with an initial aim of bringing Japanese students to New Zealand to have an English-based overseas education; and the second is that, as *taiko* has its cultural roots in Japan, it is probable that Japanese may be attracted to an art form that is familiar to them. One of the remarkable characteristics of most of the *taiko* players at IPC is that they usually have had no prior experience of playing *taiko* before coming to New Zealand. Furthermore, several of the members have continued to play *taiko* after graduating from the College, some staying in New Zealand, but most returning to Japan.

The theme of cultural exchange permeates many of the reasons students at IPC gave as to why they play *taiko*. The founder of the group, who was and still is known as "Prince" (real name: Nagao Yoshiaki), stressed that cultural exchange was an important motive for him in being involved in *taiko* at IPC.[6] Cultural exchange for Prince and many other players (former and current) seems to be based on promoting Japanese culture through *taiko* in the New Zealand context. That is, they aim to perform to the wider New Zealand public with the intention of showcasing a Japanese performing art which is perceived as traditional (although *taiko* playing in such an ensemble and choreographed setting is actually quite a modern phenomenon).[7] A flyer from a South Island tour in 2006 summarizes this premise:

> The International Pacific College (IPC) Kodama Drum Team was established in 1990 when the college opened, and is organised by the students with the support of the college and the community. The drum team consists of not only Japanese students but also students of other nationalities, plus local people. We proactice [sic] twice weekly for two hours at time. We put a lot of effort and time in improving our skills so that we can share this sophisticated Japanese culture with people of different nationalities.[8]

The notion of culture exchange is problematized when one Japanese player stressed her objective of showing *taiko* to New Zealanders as a "traditional" object, yet emphasized that if she were in Japan she would not want to play the drums. It is possible that the Japanese players, for whom the genre is relatively new, feel more comfortable playing and performing publicly to a New Zealand audience that knows very little, if anything at all, about the genre. Indeed, *taiko* is rare in New Zealand, and being under the Kiwi gaze perhaps gives the players a sense of identity: uniqueness as short-term visitors to a foreign country, yet based at an educational institution that has an immense Japanese influence: "People are very curious to watch our performance because . . . [it] is quite rare and most of people have never seen . . . our performance." While culture exchange is stressed as a bottom-up notion by the players themselves, IPC actually has a philosophy of championing cultural awareness. The College even names their *taiko* group in its Charter, as it "has gained national recognition in its performances at civic and cultural functions."[9]

---

[6] Nagao Yoshiaki, e-mail messages to author via IPC staff, 2009.

[7] See further Alaszewska, "Kumi-daiko."

[8] Kodama, e-mail message forwarded to author, June 29, 2006.

[9] International Pacific College, "III: Contribution to New Zealand's Identity and Economic, Social and Cultural Development," *Charter*, 2008, http://www.ipc.ac.nz/ charter/page_3.php.

The Japanese members of this group appear to be finding their cultural roots in New Zealand through culture exchange. For them, being Japanese in New Zealand is supported by the idea of playing a perceived traditional art form; to be a *taiko* player in New Zealand means becoming Japanese; and for *taiko* players this means cultural exchange; a way to find their roots.

## Conclusion

What does it mean to be a *taiko* player in New Zealand? While the perspective of each individual is unique to that person, the practice of *taiko* playing in New Zealand is inherently linked to group music-making and the formation of identity and culture. For these individuals and the groups in which they play, *taiko* performance is a social and cultural activity that not only partly contributes to making them what and who they are, but also ultimately helps them to shape society and culture.[10]

For New Zealand's ethnically diverse *taiko* players, to play these instruments in the New Zealand setting means several things. First and foremost, it means indexing Japan in one way or another. Players literally and metaphorically "drum up" Japan by borrowing and imitating aspects of a recently invented genre of Japanese music, drawing on the skills of invited and visiting *taiko* players to New Zealand.

Being a *taiko* player in New Zealand does not mean that the players have to be Japanese. However, for the nine *taiko* groups active in New Zealand, whether mostly Japanese, led by Japanese, or established by Japanese, ethnicity still often maintains an influencing presence that offers a sense of authenticity.

For New Zealand's *taiko* players, meaning is also attached to the importance of choreography, making drums, meeting new people, making new friends, and the sheer enjoyment of public performance: putting Japan on display; displaying New Zealand today. As one might expect, there are several underpinning reasons for playing *taiko* in New Zealand. For many players, drumming means being Japanese or becoming Japanese. It is here that notions of ethnicity, culture, and identity sometimes become interwoven and complex: they help to show some tropes on the one hand, yet problematize them on the other.

---

[10] Cf. Anthony Giddens, *The Constitution of Society: Outline of the Theory of Structuration* (Cambridge: Polity Press in association with Blackwell Publishers, 1984).

In conclusion, to return to the question posed at the start of this paper, being a *taiko* player in New Zealand can mean several things; some individual and others collective. While this discussion has identified several ideas in connection with this creative activity, being a *taiko* player in New Zealand predominantly means expressing or performing ethnicity, and ultimately helping to shape identity, society, and culture.

# References

Alaszewska, Jane. "Kumi-daiko." In *Grove Music Online. Oxford Music Online*, 2008, http://www.oxfordmusiconline.com/subscriber/article/grove /music/49402.

Clifford, James. *The Predicament of Culture: Twentieth-Century Ethnography, Literature, and Art*. Cambridge: Harvard University Press, 1988.

de Ferranti, Hugh. "Japan Beating: The Making and Marketing of Professional Taiko Music in Australia." In *Popular Culture, Globalization and Japan*, edited by Matthew Allen and Rumi Sakamoto, 75–93. New York: Routledge, 2006.

Fujie, Linda. "Japanese Taiko Drumming in International Performance: Converging Musical Ideas in the Search for Success on Stage." *The World of Music* 43, nos. 2–3 (2001): 93–101.

Giddens, Anthony. *The Constitution of Society: Outline of the Theory of Structuration*. Cambridge: Polity Press in association with Blackwell Publishers, 1984.

Hennessy, Sarah. "'Taiko SouthWest': Developing a 'New' Musical Tradition in English Schools." *International Journal of Music Education* 23, no. 3 (2005): 217–25.

International Pacific College, "III: Contribution to New Zealand's Identity and Economic, Social and Cultural Development," *Charter*, 2008, http://www.ipc.ac.nz/charter/page_3.php.

Izumi, Masumi. "Reconsidering Ethnic Culture and Community: A Case Study on Japanese Canadian Taiko Drumming." *Journal of Asian American Studies* 4, no. 1 (2001): 35–56.

Johnson, Henry. "Musical Moves and Transnational Grooves: Education, Transplantation and Japanese *Taiko* Drumming at The International Pacific College, New Zealand." In *Recentring Asia: Histories, Encounters, Identities*, edited by Jacob Edmond, Henry Johnson, and Jacqueline Leckie (Folkestone: Global Oriental, in press).

—. "Why *Taiko*? Understanding *Taiko* Performance at New Zealand's 1st *Taiko* Festival." *Sites: A Journal of Social Anthropology and Cultural Studies* 5, no. 2 (2008): 111–34.

Morris-Suzuki, Tessa. *Re-inventing Japan: Time, Space, Nation.* Armonk: M.E. Sharpe, 1998.

Wong, Deborah A. "Noisy Intersection: Ethnicity, Authenticity and Ownership in Asian American Taiko." In *Diasporas and Interculturalism in Asian Performing Arts: Translating Traditions,* edited by Hae-kyung Um, 75–90. New York: RoutledgeCurzon, 2005.

—. *Speak it Louder: Asian Americans Making Music.* New York: Routledge, 2004.

Yoon, Paul Jong Chul. "'She's Really Become Japanese Now!': Taiko Drumming and Asian American Identifications." *American Music* 19, no. 4 (2001): 417–38.

Figure 5-1. Kodama performing outside Swan House, International Pacific College, New Zealand, around 2007. Courtesy of Nishimura Tomoyo.

# CHAPTER SIX

# PRODUCING MULTIPLE VOICES:
# PATHWAYS FROM HOME TO STAGE

# ALISON BOOTH

This paper examines the role of academics in producing world music events. The study develops project network maps that focus on events that were produced at The University of Auckland during the ten year period from 1994 to 2004. The project maps highlight five events during that time which involved performances featuring traditions from Asia, as shown in Table 6-1.

In addition to event analysis, this study introduces the first stage in my development of a methodology that graphically represents the dynamics of event production, as well as generating quantitative data about those events and the relationships that enabled them. The developing model identifies and analyzes the drivers, relationships, and resources that underlie events by illustrating events as networks. I have considered current academic event theories; including stakeholder relationship circles, as developed by Allen et al., and O'Toole and Mikolaitis.[1]

In considering the role of academics involved in event production, specific issues arise. Unique research interests place some academics in positions to access performers from particular cultures or regions, or they may also be the targets of marketing efforts by foreign artists seeking performance opportunities. Just as importantly, academics have potential access to event resources through institutional infrastructure and networks. The size and relationship of their project to the larger environment and strategic policies of their university have a direct effect on their access to

---

[1] Johnny Allen et al., *Festival and Special Event Management* (Milton: John Wiley and Sons, 2002); William O'Toole and Phyllis Mikolaitis, *Corporate Event Project Management* (New York: John Wiley and Sons, 2002).

these resources. Some universities are able to offer more resources than others. Access to those resources that do exist may depend on many factors that include the position of the academic initiating the event and the size and political position of the initial academic unit, as well as the academic's networks within academia and wider spheres.

If the performers are linked to the research interest area of an academic, the academic may have greater motivation to be involved in the project and produce it within a specific department or discipline. Even with such shared cultural interests between academics and performers, a language or area specialist of the same culture as the performers may produce quite a different event than an ethnomusicologist.

Ethnomusicologists normally have areas of focussed interest, as do area and language specialists, but they are often more supportive of music performances in general. Event involvement motivation may not be solely based on research interests; it may also involve personal friendships or a university's strategic direction.

Events offer promotional opportunities and also have the capacity to create positioning for universities by reinforcing or developing global networks. Successful events have the potential to grow dynamic networks between universities and local government, as well as with local and international communities. Unsuccessful events may create financial risks as well as generate negative publicity.

## Methodology

This study develops a graphic representation of quantitative and qualitative information by using space, shape, and position to display information about world music events. When produced within academia, these can often be quite complex and may involve large and diverse project networks.

Quantitative data can be extracted by comparing drivers and interactions with types of resources accessed and types of relationships. Qualitative data is graphically illustrated by project network maps that identify three components: drivers, resources, and relationships. Drivers are those who undertake the development of the event. Resources are all the elements that make the event possible (these may include performers, funding, venues and public relations). Relationships are interests shared by drivers and resources, and may be direct or indirect. The value of this model is that the project map graphically represents the networks that connect drivers and resources, allowing projects to proceed. I introduce the graphic representation of these connections in a conceptual network map below (fig. 6-1).

Production drivers are the people who are motivated to produce an event. Drivers are represented by grey ovals placed inside resource boxes. Each driver is identified by a letter inside the oval. In projects with multiple drivers, drivers are differentiated as "A," "B," etc. Drivers are further distinguished in terms of their academic, cultural, or professional roles. Driver motivation is an issue requiring further research and is therefore beyond the scope of this study. In the network map, the placement of the driver is significant as those drivers in central positions are indicated to be of more vital importance to the event management.

Project resources are identified by rectangular boxes. Production drivers enclosed in rectangular boxes have direct access to the project resources indicated by that box. In this model there are six types of resources, labelled according to their source: university, New Zealand government agencies, foreign government agencies, performers, non-government resources, and event support. Each type has the potential to contribute a variety of valuable project assets, as indicated in Table 6-2.

One of the central features of the project network map is the identification of the relationships that unite project elements. Relationships are based on shared interests and may connect individuals as well as institutions. Furthermore, relationships between two individuals may then generate a subsequent relationship involving the institution of which one of them is a member. Fundamentally, I argue that it is these relationships that help a project driver access the potential contributions that various resources may make to the project. There are four relationship types that link drivers and resources used in this model, as outlined in Table 6-3.

Relationships unite drivers with other project participants by opening access to project resources through shared interests. Resources may also be connected by relationships to project drivers which are direct or indirect. To introduce the complexities of this model, I have included a generic academic-based world music event project map to help clarify the intricacies involved in such productions, before applying this model to the case studies included in this paper. The following conceptual map demonstrates how the project map tool is applied.

Driver A is an academic at university one. Driver B is an academic at university two, who has access to international musicians. Drivers A and B share academic research interests in world music and B has access through cultural production networks to C. C is a non-government resource providing sponsorship. B also has access through cultural production networks to event support resources with the arts venue. The arts venue has access to community trust funding. C shares cultural identity relationships with local as well as international performers and with foreign government agencies. International musicians have a commercial relationship with the local arts festival through cultural production relationships with Driver B. C has an indirect relationship to Driver A through a commercial relationship with university one. Driver A and the venue have a cultural production relationship with a local government cultural funding body, which is currently supporting the specific culture involved through funding and advocacy.

When applying project maps to different performance events, relationship clusters form patterns that help the understanding of the nature of interconnected project relationships between drivers and resources. As an introduction to the issues considered in the production of world music in New Zealand, I offer a simple example: The Ketchak! Project (fig. 6-2).

The Ketchak! Project was produced within The University of Auckland's School of Music by Ethnomusicology staff, with participation from students as well as from the local community. The six-week workshop culminated in a public performance in the School of Music Theatre.

Driver A was the sole driver and is located in the centre of this chart. The driver's location within the university provided direct access to staff with Indonesian cultural skills, financial resources from the department, administrative support, and access to venues.

The community performer resource box is linked to Driver A through a shared interest in cultural production. New Zealand cultural production relationships link individuals as well as institutions together. Student performers share Driver A's academic interests through their university study; A has an academic relationship with Balinese Dancer through academic research interests. These are direct relationships. This example includes an indirect relationship between Balinese Dancer and the university, as their financial contract creates an indirect commercial relationship to A.

Ketchak! offered participants an opportunity to take part in a performance experience outside their own culture. Such projects have the potential to create new audiences for world music through concert attendance, student recruitment, curriculum development, and university strategic positioning.

The next network map explores the multi-event project of Ashok Roy, the late Hindustani classical musician then located in Australia (fig. 6-3). Ashok Roy toured New Zealand through an academic network, performing as well as teaching workshops. Central to this project was the combination of academic and cultural drivers. Three academic drivers were involved, activating the resources of their universities to produce events that complemented the Auckland event in the national context and that supplemented the performer's income.

This example illustrates the heightened complexities of such multi-event projects. An indirect relationship is created when drivers connect to resources that they cannot access directly by taking advantage of their existing relationships with others who have the ability to access those resources.

Driver A had specific academic research interests in Roy's music culture and academic relationships with C, D, and E who provided resources from the other university events that were part of the larger project. Driver B (Kalaranjani, a charitable trust) had access to Creative New Zealand (hereafter, CNZ) funding that was not accessible to Driver A. At this time, CNZ supported community performances that represented the growing multi-ethnic migrant population.

Kalaranjani (B) supported and promoted Indian classical music from 1995 to 2000 by providing community support and access to CNZ grants that, during this period, were available for such community cultural organizations. CNZ subsidised concerts and workshops and provided travel funds within New Zealand. In this project/production, CNZ (through Kalaranjani) supported travel to the additional event locations. With direct access to this governmental funding, Kalaranjani took on the financial risks of this project. Driver A, on the other hand, had access to public relations resources controlled by The University of Auckland.

Another important feature of this graph is the relationship between Driver A and the Aotea Centre that enabled this project to gain access to this important venue. The Aotea Centre also provided production support and additional publicity for the event in their venue. They provided their services at reduced community rates that reflected management commitments to support community performing art ventures, as was then part of their mission. Driver A also had academic research links with the Hamilton Indian Community and the Gandhi Centre. B shares cultural identity lines with these two resources, as well as with the performers.

The 1997 T.N. Krishnan and N. Rajam Violin Tour illustrates a multi-event project with indirect access to international funds (fig. 6-4). These acclaimed Indian classical violinists toured New Zealand giving concerts and workshops. They were accompanied by two percussionists from India. The magnitude of this project required support beyond the capacities of university and Kalaranjani resources.

Because of the status of these performers, this project had indirect access to funds from the Indian Council for Cultural Relations (New Delhi). Consequently, this example demonstrates the final resource category in the network map model. International funding provided the performers with their international air fares and covered fees for other necessities, including visas. Direct access to internal funding was obtained by B (with the technical expertise of A) through a CNZ grant that provided enough funding to support a nationwide tour, including subsidized performance and workshop fees, internal airfares, accommodation, and *per diems*.

The Beauty of Chinese Melody introduces the relationship of universities and patronage (fig. 6-5). As a member of the production team and an audience member, I observed that the 2000-strong audience at this free concert was 90% comprised of Chinese-New Zealanders, including recent migrants to Auckland who identified to a lesser or greater extent with their Chinese heritage. The event attracted the interest of the local Chinese press, and proved to be so popular that it was moved, two weeks before the concert, from the original 450-seat venue to one that accommodated 2250 seats. The ability to fill the hall so effectively, as well as to negotiate the venue change and put in place a public relations strategy, was only possible due to the presence of the patron and his existing relationship with the university and the venue. The relationship between the patron and university continued for other projects over the next couple of years.

Drivers A, B and C dominate the centre of the chart. A and B are world-music-oriented academics with academic interests in the performers; B had access to a well-known performance group who rarely performs outside of China; and C is a private sponsor with strong Chinese cultural network lines that dominate the right-hand side of this map.

This map demonstrates how a relationship based on shared cultural identity between a driver and performance artists can be significant in expanding the networks that design how a concert is produced. It also illustrates how different relationship dynamics are created when drivers with academic interests in their research culture combine with drivers who are interested in promoting their specific culture.

The cultural identity ties accessed by C created an opportunity for a new audience at the Arts Centre that was dominated by the Chinese general public as well as by government officials. This is in strong contrast to A's academic, production, and commercial lines that supported the production side of the project. A contributed indirectly through ASB Trust Community Access funds accessed by the Aotea Centre. Additional resources were supplied by The University of Auckland, with B providing indirect funding through a performance project presented at Wellington's International Festival of the Arts.

The Korean Shaman Project was another multi-event project with driver access to financial support from international funding bodies as well as through local sponsorship (fig. 6-6). The event combines two drivers (one an academic, the other a professional working within the same university unit), opening quite different access to resources and project relationships.

Driver A combined a Korean cultural identity with research interests in Korean studies. This established relationships with and access to Korean performers, business sponsors, and diplomats. These resources provided direct as well as indirect financial resources which provided project funding. Driver B provided professional links to resources (such as academics, venues and government agencies) through established cultural production networks and experience. The specialised nature of this project and the specific skills required of the two drivers in order to deliver such a complex multi-event production are illustrated in this project map model.

This example highlights the way that different kinds of relationships can cluster around different drivers. Driver A dominates one side with academic/research and cultural identity, while B dominates the other side with New Zealand Cultural Networks. Relationship clusters highlight how drivers through relationships bring direct and indirect resources into performance projects. As this model develops, I hope to extract further information as it is revealed through relationship clusters.

## Conclusion

The visual representation of successful world music events in New Zealand during a particular period in this country's performing arts history offers important perspectives on that history. The country's academics and their institutions have acted as irreplaceable project drivers, but have also used their positions and their research skills to embed world music performers and other non-academic project drivers within production networks that have made these events possible. Equally importantly, the academics in these projects (by virtue of their multicultural experiences) have been able to connect both performers and drivers to what must still be considered mainstream New Zealand audiences.

This methodology, which I have developed and will continue to work on, is based on graphic analysis of cultural identities, relationships, and resources. It begins the process of developing a clearer understanding of the mechanics of producing New Zealand's multiple voices and presenting them to that audience.

# References

Allen, Johnny, William O'Toole, Ian McDonnell, and Robert Harris. *Festival and Special Event Management*. Milton: John Wiley and Sons, 2002.

O'Toole, William, and Phyllis Mikolaitis. *Corporate Event Project Management*. New York: John Wiley and Sons, 2002.

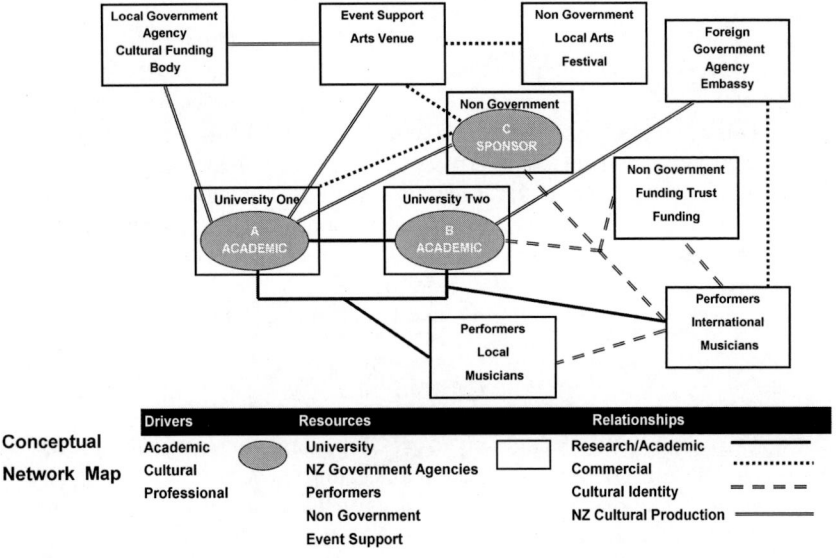

Figure 6-1.

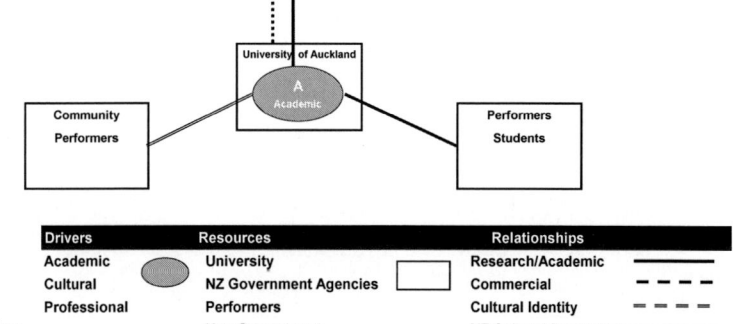

Figure 6-2.

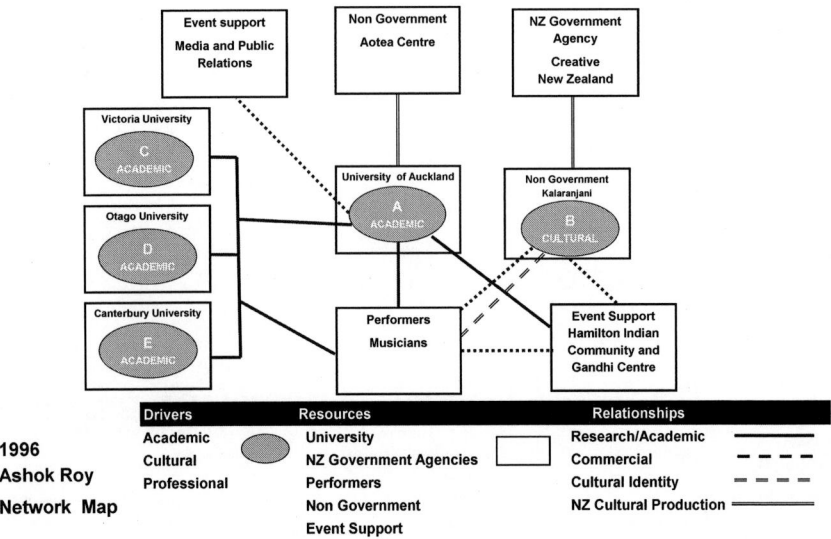

Figure 6-3.

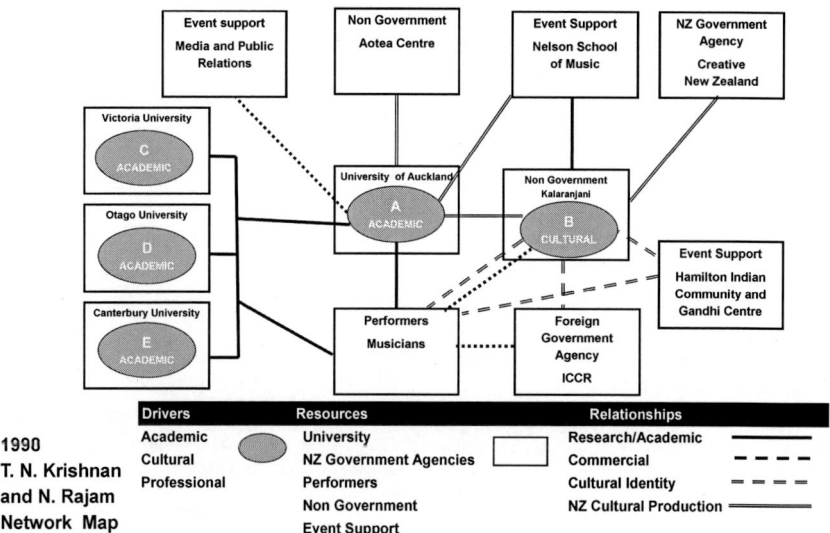

1990
T. N. Krishnan
and N. Rajam
Network Map

Figure 6-4.

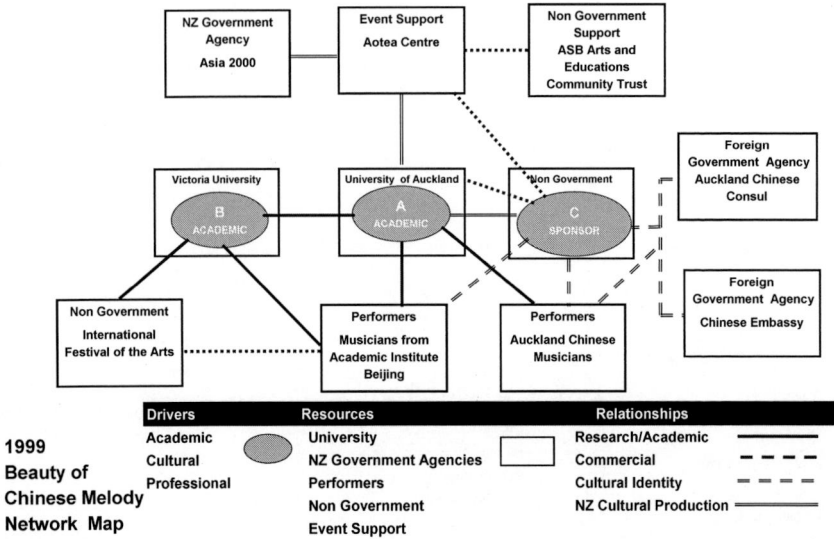

Figure 6-5.

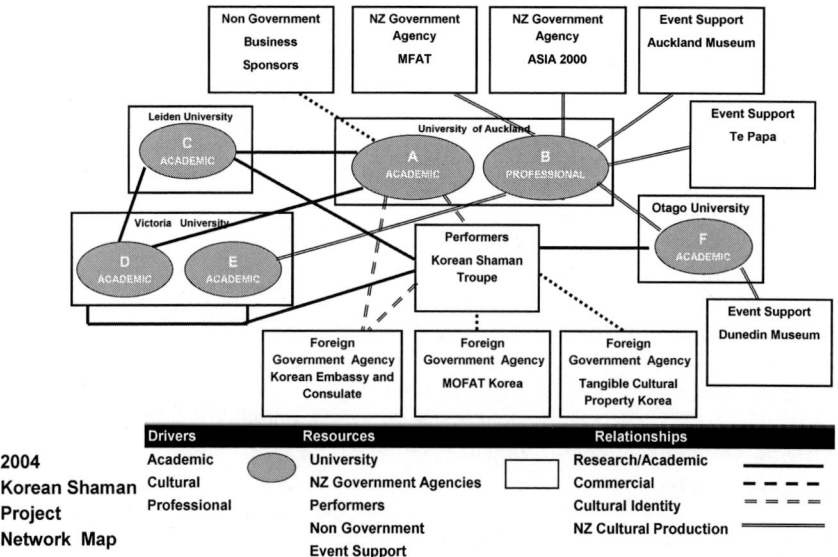

Figure 6-6.

## Table 6-1. Performance Projects 1994–2004

| Year | Event |
|------|-------|
| 1994 | Ketchak! (Bali) |
| 1996 | Ashok Roy (North India) |
| 1997 | T.N. Krishnan and N. Rajam (South and North India) |
| 1998 | The Beauty of Chinese Melody (China) |
| 2004 | Korean Shaman Project (Korea) |

**Table 6-2. Project Resource Contributions**

| Sector | Contribution |
| --- | --- |
| University | Cultural skill |
| | Administration |
| | Legal |
| | Financial |
| | Venue |
| | Promotion |
| New Zealand | Financial |
| Government Agencies | Access to other government agency resources |
| | Legal |
| Foreign Government | Grants and sponsorship funds |
| Agencies | Legal |
| Performers | Event content |
| | Intangibles (reputation, cultural capital, networks) |
| Non Government | Financial |
| | Community networks and volunteers |
| Event Support | Promotional design and distribution |
| | Production details including media, venue, advertising, ticketing, audience, technical, front and back of house |

**Table 6-3. Relationship Lines**

| Relationship Type | Key |
| --- | --- |
| Research and Academic | Solid Line |
| Commercial | Dotted Line |
| Shared Cultural Identity | Broken Line |
| New Zealand Cultural Production Networks | Double Line |

# PART II:

# POPULAR CULTURE

# CHAPTER SEVEN

## OUR STREET:
## PERFORMING POLITICS AND IDENTITY
## IN MT. ROSKILL

### KIRSTEN ZEMKE

"Deep in Auckland's inner city beats a vibrant multi-ethnic heart and this is what *Our Street* celebrates."[1]

This paper explores multiple layers and discourses around the identity of a suburb in Auckland, New Zealand, as expressed and negotiated in an original musical theatre production entitled *Our Street*. I argue that this project offers a comprehensive, vital, and heterogeneous notion of a contemporary urban New Zealand identity which includes diversity of ethnicity, religion, gender, and experience.

Billed in promotional material as a diverse musical theatre performance which showcased various arts including krumping, hip hop, animation, and the thirty-three piece Ikuna Tongan Youth Brass Band, it also featured a local Somalian documentary project and an Indian-New Zealand theatre group (Prayas). The Auckland City Council identified Wesley as a neighbourhood that would benefit from intercultural theatre, so it funded the *Our Street* production which was performed five times in the city centre at the Auckland Town Hall on August 13–16, 2008. It was directed by Justine Simei-Barton and I had the privilege of being a musical director and composer for the show, paralleling another City Council project Justine and I worked on twenty years previously, which had launched the Pacific Island Theatre Group. I wrote a few original songs for the project, and helped nurture, choose, and develop a number of other songs, incidental music, and dance beds with D. Kamali (music director and band mentor), the director, the cast, and the musicians.

---

[1] Michael Field, "Review: *Our Street* in Auckland," *Stuff,* August 15, 2008, http://www.stuff.co.nz/entertainment/582352.

Simonett states that music and dance are a means by which a community appears as a community, to itself.[2] In this article, I examine this music drama event in light of Simonett's statement; showing how this particular New Zealand street asserted its inclusive, layered, contemporary identity through music and dance.

Papastergiadis asserts that "traditional notions of the local often fail to capture the specific details of community life" and says that "national structures are not flexible enough to accommodate the breadth and diversity of cultural affiliations."[3] *Our Street* offers an engagement through music and dance with the varied and contested identities that were enmeshed in the experiences of residents of a single street, McGehan Close in Mt. Roskill, Auckland. The Labour-held Mt. Roskill electorate has the highest percentage of ethnic Asians of any general electorate, and only 46 percent of this electorate were born in New Zealand (the lowest of any electorate).[4]

Because music and dance are socially grounded, they are terrain for political experience.[5] McGehan Close had previously featured infamously in a "state of the nation speech" by National Party leader, John Key (leader of the opposition at the time, now Prime Minister). Mr Key stated that there were "streets in our country where helplessness has become ingrained . . . dead ends for those who live in them . . . places where rungs on the ladder of opportunity have been broken. I'm talking about streets like McGehan Close."[6]

After public outcry from the residents, Key visited McGehan Close and publicly took twelve-year-old resident Aroha Ireland to Waitangi Day celebrations. Ireland was not in the play but a few of her neighbours were. This street had become a weapon for National to attack the Labour Party, and part of the function of this theatre project was to reply to Key's accusation of helplessness.

---

[2] Helena Simonett, "Popular Music and the Politics of Identity: The Empowering Sound of Technobanda," *Popular Music and Society* 24, no. 2 (2000): 1–23.

[3] Nikos Papastergiadis, "Hybridity and Ambivalence: Place and Flows on Contemporary Art Culture," *Theory, Culture and Society* 22, no. 4 (2005): 55.

[4] "Mt. Roskill Electorate Profile," *New Zealand Parliament Website*, http://www.parliament.nz/NR/rdonlyres/7E66E5EE–77BD–4419–932C-0F382FFC436B/77906/MtRoskill_profile_5.pdf.

[5] Simonett, "Popular Music and the Politics of Identity," 1–23.

[6] Hon. John Key, "The Kiwi Way: A Fair Go for All. A State of the Nation Speech" (Speech given at the Burnside Rugby Clubrooms, Christchurch, New Zealand, January 30, 2007), http://www.national.org.nz/Article.aspx?ArticleID=9215.

Close to McGehan Close is the Wesley Community Centre where many of the performers and artists were drawn from, giving the show a broader "suburb" identity. The Wesley, Mt. Roskill, Mt. Albert, and Blockhouse Bay areas of Auckland city contain at least eighty different ethnic groups, of which Papua New Guinean, Somalian, Māori, Indian, Pākehā, Samoan, and Tongan were specifically presented in the show.

This range of "outsider" (and indigenous) national identities was explored in the context of one contemporary Auckland neighbourhood, in a piece which included significant migrant themes of journey and belonging. The endorsement by the Auckland City Council gives the project the status of being artistically representative of Auckland city. One reviewer claimed, "there is something uniquely Auckland to see a young Indian girl performing a Polynesian Dance; and Auckland PI kids doing Bollywood."[7]

Auckland, the largest city in Aotearoa, is a distinct but statistically dominant component of any constructions or articulations of a New Zealand identity. I show how additional identity layers—such as gender, religion, and age—intersect these geographically-based identities.

Papastergiadis has a problem with the arrogance in the notion that "members of indigenous societies, whose knowledge systems have been violently dismantled by colonialism, are now lacking the capacity to confront the challenges of contemporary life."[8] *Our Street* is a musical exploration, confrontation, and arbitration with varied notions of identity, providing an example of indigenous and minority peoples using music to deal with their challenges and defining and dismantling hegemonic national and city identities.

The narrative, and much of the dialogue and action of the play, was derived from weeklong "intensives." During these workshops, poetry, raps, and stories emerged that were incorporated into the script. The story, centred on a particular *cul de sac*, was negotiated by the participants to represent probable or actual situations from that neighbourhood, including cultures they came across, gangs and crime, and not feeling cohesion or unity in the neighbourhood. The narrative focused on two neighbouring homes, one Indian and one Samoan, where the eldest daughters were getting married. The drama stemmed from difficulties in the romantic relationships, family pressures, and ethnic differences, and fixed around the homework project of a young high-school student writing about her "world." Many of the performers and musical items emerged from

---

[7] Field, "Review: *Our Street* in Auckland."
[8] Papastergiadis, "Hybridity and Ambivalence," 48.

performing arts groups based at the Wesley Community Centre. This was the grounds for the show's inclusion of hip hop dance, Somalian film-making, graphic arts (in the set), the Indian theatre group, the Tongan Brass band, and the young reggae band (BOW—Band of Wesley) which backed the live performances. All of these arts were taught and or practised at the local community centre, so the inclusion of this variety of cultures and styles was an organic reflection of actual arts practised in that neighbourhood, rather than any fictional hopes or ideals of the writers and director.

Papastergiadis posits that migration and displacement irretrievably alter ideas of home and nation, and these are articulated on two levels: in the production of artworks, and within the identity of artists.[9] The closing song of *Our Street* (sung in English, Hindi, and Samoan) reified this altered notion of home with an assertion of belonging, neighbourhood, and acceptance: "This is our street, this is our home, we all belong, this is our world." The play on "world" highlights the international cultures and journeys expressed as well as the localized identity and belonging. Migration was highlighted in the opening item of *Our Street,* which depicted through dance the frigate bird which, according to Māori legend, guides people to the shores of Aotearoa. The reality of artists with multiple national identities and alignments was articulated in another musical item, which depicted the journey of the protagonist's ancestors from Samoa and Great Britain. It featured a Pacific chant (*Nga poraka*) overlaid with "My Bonnie lies over the Ocean," which surprisingly worked musically and was accompanied by Samoan style dance and canoe paddling moves.

Traditional Pacific dance styles were integrated organically into the narrative—with some young girls rehearsing a dance item for a wedding. This highlights one of the contexts for traditional Pacific dance in urban New Zealand life—it is performed for family events and celebrations, and fits in with other pursuits like school, jobs, etc. Turino claims that dance, because of its complex imagery, can articulate better than speech the complexity and tensions of history and life, and is more able to transcend "rationalist" discourse.[10] A significant moment in the story which used dance was when a mother was attacking her future son-in-law for getting another girl pregnant and, instead of dialogue, this was performed in dance. The mother was Samoan and she used Samoan spear moves, the

---

[9] Papastergiadis, "Hybridity and Ambivalence," 55.

[10] Thomas Turino, *Moving Away from Silence: Music of the Peruvian Altiplano and the Experience of Urban Migration* (Chicago: University of Chicago Press, 1993), 95.

groom responded with a *haka* of shame and apology as he was Māori, and nearby Samoan female supporters performed gentle *maululu* dance moves to calm the situation and pull the mother away. The band started with the Samoan *siva* song when the Samoan girls danced in for the joyous wedding, but shifted to a plaintive electric guitar solo for the conflict— signifying rage, pain, contemporary life, and masculinity.

Popular African-American dance and music styles (krump, hip hop, step, and reggae) arguably no longer signify as foreign or American in Aotearoa, but have come to be a common feature of Pacific and Māori community aesthetics and performance.[11] Osumare found that "international meanings of black identity, signified through hip hop, compound issues of race and power relations when filtered through various other countries' issues of marginality and difference."[12] Hip hop and reggae have been embraced and appropriated by Pacific and Māori artists for the last thirty years and represent cultural and political alignments as well as an aesthetic choice.[13] Krump and step dance are African-American dance styles related to hip hop that have seeped into Aotearoa. Learned through a combination of observing movies and videos, and oral transmission, Pacific and Māori youth—particularly in south and west Auckland—have become proficient in these practises. They were incorporated into this narrative, utilized for their expressive and emotive powers. For instance, the krumping was staged as a battle between opposing groups, using dance to represent the conflict, in place of action or dialogue. Battling is a thematic characteristic of krumping, which employs mock, virtuoso, and competitive battles. Osumare talks about an "inter-cultural body," where street practitioners of all nationalities negotiate complex identities, cutting and pasting a potpourri of global cultures "in the moment," through their bodies.[14]

The BOW band accompanied the whole show live on stage. They were mostly high-school aged students, from Fijian, Cook Island, and Tongan backgrounds, who, under the tutelage of Daren Kamali, have been part of

---

[11] Kirsten Zemke-White, "Keeping it Real (Indigenous): Hip Hop in Aotearoa as Community, Culture and Consciousness," in *Cultural Studies in Aotearoa New Zealand: Identity, Space and Place*, ed. Claudia Bell and Steve Matthewman (Melbourne: Oxford University Press, 2004), 205–28.

[12] Halifu Osumare, "Beat Streets in the Gobal Hood: Connective Marginalities of the Hip Hop Globe," *Journal of American & Comparative Cultures* 24, nos. 1–2 (2008): 171–81.

[13] Zemke-White, "Keeping it Real (Indigenous)," 205–28.

[14] Halifu Osumare, "Global Breakdancing and the Intercultural Body," *Dance Research Journal* 34, no. 2 (2002): 30–45.

a music project of the Wesley Community Centre. The Auckland City Council provided musical instruments and sound gear, and employed poet and rapper Kamali to offer musical instruction. The BOW's primary interest was reggae, in fact it was a challenge to expand their horizons to the other musical styles of the show. Manuel and Marchall describe reggae's movement from Jamaica as an "efflorescence of the kind of musical creativity accompanying a broader condition of post-modern, secondary orality embracing new technologies."[15] This postmodern orality has led to reggae being a very popular music style in islands across the Pacific. There were two reggae songs in the show.

The BOW band had to engage with "Bollywood," India's pop music, which comes almost exclusively from song dance numbers in films. A contested term, "Bollywood" as a word was accepted by the Indian participants and, as a play on words, captures the global orientation of this pop culture. Bollywood is a transnational phenomenon which, Gopal and Moorti argue, will always be shaped by the specific sites of its emergence; whether in diaspora or non-Indian versions.[16] The whole cast, all of the cultures involved, danced on stage to the Bollywood-style song we composed.

Gender should be taken into consideration in any exploration of identity. Valdez and Halley found that patriarchy can often be present in both traditional and hegemonic music cultures and therefore diaspora musics are an area where conventional gender identities and inequalities often continue to be reproduced.[17] *Our Street*, however, saw women dominate in the narrative and in the organization of the performance. The director, producer, dramaturge, and the composer (myself) were all women. The story centred on a young school girl and the families the drama was based on were both headed by women who were involved in the marriages of their daughters. There was a strong Samoan grandmother character and an old woman of mysterious ethnic origin who played a solo piano piece.

This piano piece, performed by Cook Island pianist Apii McKinley, begins with the lonely, eccentric migrant woman playing a medley of the various musics she hears on the street (reggae, Indian pop, and hip hop, integrated with European classical music). The piece then moves into the

---

[15] Peter Manuel and Wayne Marshall, "The Riddim Method: Aesthetics, Practice, and Ownership in Jamaican Dancehall," *Popular Music* 25, no. 3 (2006): 467.

[16] Sangita Gopal and Sujata Moorti, *Global Bollywood: Travels of Hindi Song and Dance* (Minneapolis, MN: University of Minnesota Press, 2008), 3.

[17] Avelardo Valdez and Jeffrey Halley, "Gender in the Culture of Mexican American Conjunto Music," *Gender & Society* 10, no. 2 (1996): 148–67.

song "Beyond the Reef,"[18] a *hapa haole* or European-influenced Hawaiian standard which has come to signify as Polynesian. Hawaiian pop music was very popular among the Pacific communities in Aotearoa in the 1940s and '50s,[19] and many second- and third-generation Pacific families in Aotearoa remember this musical era fondly. A talented young performer danced a hula to this piano medley, signifying an idealized Polynesia, nostalgia, sexuality, and history. This also highlights the notion of age and identity, acting as a foil to the mostly youthful music and diaspora stories of the rest of the play.

There were only two solo songs presented, one of which was performed by a young girl pregnant out of wedlock. Her plaintive R'n'B solo described her feelings around the pregnancy, discussed her choices, and lamented that her parents were in another country. The use of the R'n'B genre reflects its great popularity in the pop charts of Aotearoa and its continued relevance and attractiveness to Pacific and Māori young people.[20] African-American R'n'B is heavily rooted in church and gospel music, and this is paralleled in Pacific communities where the church is the centre of religious, cultural, family, and community life. While contemporary R'n'B may be transferred along mass-mediated airwaves, Pacific people have grasped its spiritual roots and arguably are attracted to it both aesthetically and culturally. The singer, Vasi Moala, was experienced in both R'n'B and gospel singing. R'n'B is thematically obsessed with romance and sex (derived from the Blues) and the use of a "love themed" R'n'B song in *Our Street* highlights the disturbances in sexuality and gender roles that migrant communities often experience, provoked by new social relations.[21]

The second solo was written and sung by BOW member Shane Akauola. Entitled "Polynesian Woman," it celebrated the beauty and desirability of Polynesian women. On the one hand, it reified stereotypes of Pacific women as seen in colonial depictions,[22] but, on the other hand, it

---

[18] Jack Pitman, "Beyond the Reef," *To You Sweetheart, Aloha*, Cadence CLP-3029/CLP-25029, 1960.

[19] Sam Sampson, "South-Sea-Island Magic—Bill Sevesi and the Auckland Music Scene," *Perfect Beat* 4, no. 1 (1998): 19–46.

[20] Kirsten Zemke-White, "Nesian Styles (Re)present R'n'B: The Appropriation, Transformation and Realization of Contemporary R'n'B with Hip Hop by Urban Pasifika Groups in Aotearoa," *Sites* 2, no. 1 (2005): 94–123.

[21] George Lipsitz, "World Cities and World Beat: Low-Wage Labor and Transnational Culture," *The Pacific Historical Review* 68 (1999): 213–32.

[22] Tamasailau Suaalii, "Deconstructing the 'Exotic' Female Beauty of the Pacific Islands," in *Bitter Sweet: Indigenous Women in the Pacific,* ed. Alison Jones,

represented the Pacific community as trying to celebrate their own looks and styles, in the face of the domination of white hegemony in relation to standards of beauty.

A further intersection to this complex neighbourhood identity is religion. The Mt. Roskill electorate has the highest percentage of Hindu (12 percent) and Muslim (6.7 percent) people out of any electorate in New Zealand.[23] The Pacific-dominated cast offered Christian prayers at the beginning of rehearsals and shows, and the Muslim Somali women involved did not appear on stage in person. There also were many Hindu in the cast, yet religion as an issue was avoided in the narrative—even though the story included weddings. Religion is perhaps presently too sensitive an area of diversity to be fully explored and acknowledged in explorations of a New Zealand identity.

Blacking and Lipsitz posit that musical change and popular musics can epitomize the changing conditions and concerns of social groups, usually before they are crystallized in other arts, national policies, or even national identities.[24] *Our Street* is a case-study of how musical performance can articulate the critical and cultural practises that have emerged in pockets of New Zealand life with complexity and innovation. Exploring through music, dance, and drama the identities and exigencies of a single Auckland street, this show negotiated multiple layers, journeys, and cultural political transactions. Music can provide a soundtrack to a shared national culture, but it can also question a patronizing and homogenizing status quo.[25] Without romanticizing intercultural dialogues, this suburban multinational, multi-experiential narrative utilized integrated globalized and indigenous musics to confront the challenges of urban life and embarked on defining a more comprehensive, accurate, and intricate identity for Aotearoa.

---

Phyllis Herda, and Tamasailau Suaalii (Dunedin: University of Otago Press, 2009), 93–108.

[23] "Mt. Roskill Electorate Profile."

[24] John Blacking, "Some Problems of Theory and Method in the Study of Musical Change," *Yearbook of the International Folk Music Council* 9 (1977): 1–26; Lipsitz, "World Cities and World Beat," 213–31.

[25] Anthony Macias, "Bringing Music to the People: Race, Urban Culture, and Municipal Politics in Postwar Los Angeles," *American Quarterly* 56, no. 3 (2004): 712.

# References

Blacking, John. "Some Problems of Theory and Method in the Study of Musical Change." *Yearbook of the International Folk Music Council* 9 (1977): 1–26.

Field, Michael. "Review: *Our Street* in Auckland." *Stuff,* August 15, 2008, http://www.stuff.co.nz/entertainment/582352.

Gopal, Sangita, and Sujata Moorti. *Global Bollywood: Travels of Hindi Song and Dance.* Minneapolis: University of Minnesota Press, 2008.

Key, Hon. John. "The Kiwi Way: A Fair Go for All: A State of the Nation Speech." Speech given at the Burnside Rugby Clubrooms, Christchurch, New Zealand, January 30, 2007, http://www.national.org.nz/ Article.aspx?ArticleID=9215.

Lipsitz, George. "World Cities and World Beat: Low-Wage Labor and Transnational Culture." *The Pacific Historical Review* 68 (1999): 213–31.

Macias, Anthony. "Bringing Music to the People: Race, Urban Culture, and Municipal Politics in Postwar Los Angeles." *American Quarterly* 56, no. 3 (2004): 693–717.

Manuel, Peter, and Wayne Marshall. "The Riddim Method: Aesthetics, Practice, and Ownership in Jamaican Dancehall." *Popular Music* 25, no. 3 (2006): 447–70.

Osumare, Halifu. "Beat Streets in the Global Hood: Connective Marginalities of the Hip Hop Globe." *Journal of American & Comparative Cultures* 24, nos. 1–2 (2008): 171–81.

—. "Global Breakdancing and the Intercultural Body." *Dance Research Journal* 34, no. 2 (2002): 30–45.

Papastergiadis, Nikos. "Hybridity and Ambivalence: Place and Flows on Contemporary Art Culture." *Theory, Culture and Society* 22, no. 4 (2005): 39–64.

Pitman, Jack. "Beyond the Reef." *To You Sweetheart, Aloha.* Cadence CLP-3029/CLP-25029, 1960.

Sampson, Sam. "South-Sea-Island Magic—Bill Sevesi and the Auckland Music Scene." *Perfect Beat* 4, no. 1 (1998): 19–46.

Simonett, Helena. "Popular Music and the Politics of Identity: The Empowering Sound of Technobanda." *Popular Music and Society* 24, no. 2 (2000): 1–21.

Suaalii, Tamasailau. "Deconstructing the 'Exotic': Female Beauty of the Pacific Islands." In *Bitter Sweet: Indigenous Women in the Pacific,* edited by Alison Jones, Phyllis Herda, and Tamasailau Suaalii, 93–108. Dunedin: University of Otago Press, 2000.

Turino, Thomas. *Moving Away from Silence: Music of the Peruvian Altiplano and the Experience of Urban Migration.* Chicago: University of Chicago Press, 1993.

Valdez, Avelardo, and Jeffrey Halley. "Gender in the Culture of Mexican American Conjunto Music." *Gender & Society* 10, no. 2 (1996): 148–67.

Zemke-White, Kirsten. "Keeping it Real (Indigenous): Hip Hop in Aotearoa as Community, Culture and Consciousness." In *Cultural Studies in Aotearoa New Zealand: Identity, Space and Place*, edited by Claudia Bell and Steve Matthewman, 205–28. Melbourne: Oxford University Press, 2004.

—. "Nesian Styles (Re)present R'n'B: The Appropriation, Transformation and Realization of Contemporary R'n'B with Hip Hop by Urban Pasifika Groups in Aotearoa." *Sites* 2, no. 1 (2005): 94–123.

CHAPTER EIGHT

"GOING OUT TO EVERYONE"?
BIC RUNGA AS A "NEW ZEALAND" ARTIST

MATTHEW BANNISTER

Since her 1997 debut, *Drive*,[1] Bic Runga has enjoyed local and
international commercial success while maintaining artistic credibility
(economic and cultural capital), and is now one of New Zealand's best-
known popular music writers/performers.[2] Despite being a non-white
woman, she has become part of the "Kiwi rock" hierarchy/canon, thereby
challenging dominant representations of New Zealand popular cultural
identity. In this essay I discuss representations of Runga in her videos and
music in terms of a negotiation with popular discourses of "Kiwi" identity,
in which non-white females are doubly marginalized. Becoming a "local
identity" necessitates consistent and credible media representations (where
"credible" means maintaining two kinds of cultural capital: both authentic
artistry and authentic locality). Representations are also "performances,"
metaphorically linking musicians as media personalities with the idea of
identity as a performance.[3] Performance is built on a tension between
audience identification and desire, or identity and difference—the
"credible" performer needs to be believable but also in some sense
exceptional, spectacular. I contend that in Runga's performances (whether
videos, songs, or live shows) this dialectic is essential to negotiating an
identity that is both Same and Other, Kiwi and exotic. Runga's marginality

---

[1] Bic Runga, *Drive,* Sony 488580.2, 1997.
[2] According to Campbell Smith, Bic Runga's manager, "Bic's three studio albums
[(all Sony, New Zealand)] have sold around half a million copies worldwide, just
under half of them outside of New Zealand." Bic Runga, *Drive*, Sony 488580.2,
1997; *Beautiful Collision,* Sony 5084039000, 2002; *Birds*, Sony 82876755532,
2005. Campbell Smith, e-mail message to author, May 6, 2009.
[3] Judith Butler, *Gender Trouble: Feminism and the Subversion of Identity* (New
York: Routledge, 1990), 25.

could be associated with a critical awareness of the performativity of identity that makes it possible to represent a dominant identity "better" than the dominant group can themselves.

New Zealand identity is a dominant discourse, based on the hegemony of white settler Pākehā values, neatly encapsulated in the popular term "Kiwi." But such identity talk is also now increasingly institutionalized in governmental creative industries policies, leading some commentators to question the uncritical way it is used.[4] Kiwi popular culture is repeatedly identified with landscape, nature, and countryside (and more recently with "clean green" environmental purity); and with farmers and practical DIY "blokes" (usually white)—all of which confirms not some myth of organic local identity, but rather Marx's insight that a society's dominant ideologies are based on its material means of production.[5] Kiwi identity is about the countryside because our economy is based on exporting raw materials (mostly plant and animal-based) and, to some degree, tourism.[6] In popular music, "Kiwi" has historically meant guitar-based pop/rock, played by groups of white men, exemplified by *Nature's Best* (note the conflation of nature and nation), a 2001 CD compilation of the top 100 New Zealand songs of all time, as chosen by Australasian Performing Rights Association members (songwriters) and released by Sony New Zealand.[7] Runga, with two entries in the Top 30 and four more in the Top 100, is the exception; a remarkable feat considering that at that time she had released just one album, *Drive*.

From the normative point of view of the heterosexual male gaze, a woman's sexuality or body tends to disrupt musical performance more than a man's.[8] Heterosexual male identity is constructed through difference: desire of the female Other and identification with the male Same. So, while male identity in culture is taken for granted, women are exceptional, in all senses of the word. The Same/Other binary is hierarchical—the latter term is devalued (e.g., man/woman, rock/pop,

---

[4] Nabeel Zuberi, "Sounds Like Us—Popular Music and Cultural Nationalism in Aotearoa/New Zealand," *Perfect Beat* 8, no. 3 (2007): 3–18.

[5] Dino Felluga, "Modules on Marx: On Ideology," in *Introductory Guide to Critical Theory,* 2005, http://www.purdue.edu/guidetotheory/marxism/modules/marxideology.html.

[6] Matthew Bannister, "Kiwi Blokes: Recontextualising Pakeha Masculinities in a Global Setting," *Genders Online* 42 (2005), http://www.genders.org/g42/g42_bannister.html.

[7] *Nature's Best,* Epic/Sony 5054952000, 2002.

[8] Lucy Green, *Music, Gender, Education* (Cambridge: Cambridge University Press, 1997), 22–26.

mind/body, reality/appearance). Dominant representations of gender in musical performance highlight women's bodies, whether as objects or as the source of their voices (e.g., the female vocalist in contradistinction to the backing band). On New Zealand's music video channel C4, although the proportion of women musicians is reasonably high, the range of representations is quite narrow: they are usually presented as vocalists, often performing solo or with other women singers, in a narrow range of genres such as pop and R'n'B. Male representations are much more diverse: they are presented as vocalists, instrumentalists, DJs, in bands, in pop, rock, and hip hop. Thus, female performers are identified with genres viewed as having less cultural capital, hence their relative exclusion from rock canons.

Another prejudice female performers must overcome is the broader cultural bias against contemporary "pop" music, as a feminized form of mass culture.[9] In the case of TrueBliss, New Zealand's version of the Spice Girls, the brief flurry of national popularity generated by the local reality TV show about the formation of the group was inevitably followed by critical vilification, group break-up, and members going on to solo careers; some as musicians with limited success (Carly Binding), but most tending towards mainstream entertainment (e.g., cabaret, Christmas in the Park, advertising, TV presenting). This is a common strategy for local female musicians (e.g., Fiona McDonald, formerly of the Headless Chickens, advertising instant noodles), but its artistic credibility or cultural capital is low. The singer/songwriter role seems more credible because of its connotations of authorship and autonomy (e.g., Shona Laing and Sharon O'Neill; and, more recently, Brooke Fraser and Anika Moa). But its "soft rock," "folksy" and confessional connotations render it marginal to masculinist rock discourse. The role highlights women as solo performers and, while the presence of an instrument lessens the connotation of sexual display, usually the instrument is acoustic as opposed to electronic; associated with natural, bodily musicality, rather than the technological and mental mastery associated with the male performer.[10] However, in the New Zealand context, the female singer/songwriter is in a relatively marketable niche as the association with the guitar brings her closer to dominant discourses of Kiwi rock.

---

[9] Andreas Huyssen, "Mass Culture as Woman: Modernism's Other," in *Studies in Entertainment: Critical Approaches to Mass Culture*, ed. Tania Modleski (Bloomington: Indiana University Press, 1986), 188–207.
[10] Green, *Music, Gender, Education*, 53, 84–85.

I have implied that the gaze is the most important means by which (gender) identity and musical performance are organized. I want to look at some of Runga's videos in this light. The video of "Sway," Runga's biggest hit, is based around a negotiation of the gaze. Performing the song on a guitar lessens the element of sexual display, and emphasizes instead her technical ability.[11] The camera looks at Runga but she does not look back, rather her gaze is directed elsewhere, towards a boy who works behind the counter in a dairy. So there is a partial reversal of the gaze, which casts Runga in the more active role of pursuer rather than object: almost a female stalker. A further implication is that her character is also an observer, an onlooker, and in some sense an outsider (she doesn't get the guy).

In the video of "Say After Me,"[12] superficially the gaze is invited through close-ups, soft illumination, a neutral background, a focus on the face and upper body, Runga's immaculate make-up and silky feminine dress. The song is an emotive, nostalgic ballad, inviting an interpretation of Runga as emotional and intimate. But there is also a distancing effect. The image is so smooth and perfect it reminds us of its performativity (reinforced by the microphone prop, and the cut-away to reveal successively a spotlight and a colour filter whirling in the background). Runga is performing, and the role she is playing is a torch singer; associated with camp artifice, masquerade and female impersonation (Dusty Springfield comes to mind). Cool blue is the predominant tone which, combined with white smoke, tends to suggest a cold night. Erotic flesh tones are absent. The overall impression is of distant melancholy (the moon), until the middle eight when a sudden eruption of fireworks seems almost kitsch or *de trop*.

If these videos renegotiate the gaze through positioning Runga as a performer and an outsider, these connotations are expanded in "Listening for the Weather" and "Get Some Sleep"—folksy road songs with videos which situate Runga in "heartland" New Zealand, both in terms of location and musical style.[13] Again the emphasis is on Runga as a performer—a working musician "on the road"—rather than an attractive object. In "Get Some Sleep," she is a DJ broadcasting from the back of a truck traveling

---

[11] Bic Runga, "Sway," *Youtube*, 1997,
http://www.youtube.com/ watch?v=w28ZREQe3_Q.
[12] Bic Bunga, "Say After Me," *Youtube*, 2006,
http://www.youtube.com/ watch?v=8WF2Js0Mc_s.
[13] Bic Runga, "Listening for the Weather," *Youtube*, 2002,
http://www.youtube.com/ watch?v=LcqbtXSlcx8; Bic Runga, "Get Some Sleep,"
*Youtube*, 2002, http://www.youtube.com/ watch?v=-C1yNyiUmF4.

through rural New Zealand, a mediated presence communicating through music, not actually making direct contact with people. In one sequence she whips out a camera, almost like a tourist, so we get the impression that while she is in the landscape she is not of it—just passing through, perhaps. The muted colour palette, low-key doco-style camerawork, and the fairly cluttered and grotty interiors tend to deglamorize, connoting down-to-earth rural honesty.

"Something Good" is also locally located (in Cuba Street Mall, Wellington), but the central conceit of the video is that Runga is a ghost— invisible and immaterial. Ordinary people and objects pass through her, though there is a subtext that emotional connections make things real.[14] Runga, while being in New Zealand, is not of it—rather, she is a performer, a star, visible to all yet also removed and distant; insular, communicating emotion and intimacy through her medium rather than directly. Then suddenly in the middle eight, the most emotionally charged part of the song, she goes airborne in the middle of Cuba Street Mall, becoming visible to all.

Runga's career has been managed to enhance her "Kiwiness," primarily through careful selection of collaborators, material, and performance contexts. Most obviously she cultivated the Kiwi rock fraternity by touring with old-timers Tim Finn and Dave Dobbyn (making the CD *Together in Concert*), thus demonstrating that she is symbolically "one of the boys" who can "cut it live."[15] She also has a long history of employing young, hip, slightly alternative local musicians as collaborators: for example, members of Pluto, Flying Nun band Bressa Creeting Cake, and Alan Gregg (ex-Mutton Birds) have featured in her touring and recording line-ups; and, more recently (on *Birds*), she worked with Neil Finn, Shayne Carter, Anika Moa, and Anna Coddington. These relationships speak of a determination to value and promote local talent. In return, they confer an aura of local authenticity upon her work. Such associations also enhance her cultural capital and artistic credibility, without unduly challenging her basically mainstream, middle-class audience. She has also been willing to experiment stylistically and take risks, in a limited way. On *Live in Concert with the Christchurch Symphony,* she performs songs by bohemian/literary singer/songwriters like Bob Dylan, Leonard Cohen, Jacques Brel, and Nick Cave; through to

---

[14] Bic Runga, "Something Good," *Youtube*, 2002, http://www.youtube.com/ watch?v=UTRk4eXxwzA.
[15] Bic Runga, Tim Finn, and Dave Dobbyn, *Together in Concert: Live*, CRA Records/Epic 5011402000, 2000.

classic pop artists like Bacharach/David and Rose Royce (significantly, her only R'n'B cover).[16] The bohemian singer/songwriter discourse enhances cultural capital, while the quasi-classical medium of orchestral concert exudes bourgeois respectability. The CD/concert presents Runga as a chanteuse, a model of mainstream artistry, while the rock references supply an "edge."[17] Her 2004 New Zealand tour used churches as venues—again this can be interpreted as subtly innovative (churches being at once mainstream and local), but also at the same time imbued with an aura which enhances perceptions of Runga's artistry; combining locality and ordinariness with "high art."[18]

In terms of musical style, Runga has stuck to classic "pop" formats that are acceptable to a mainstream middle-class New Zealand audience. But within these parameters she has also been quite exploratory, ranging from guitar-based folky pop, the musical style that connotes locality most clearly to a Pākehā audience, to classic '60s-style middle-of-the-road pop balladry à la Dusty Springfield or Dionne Warwick, and to bohemian songwriter/auteurs (e.g. Dylan and Cohen). She tends to avoid styles that are obviously contemporary, because of the risk (especially for a female performer) of being branded as "trendy" or commercial. She did experiment with drum'n'bass rhythms for her second album, but dropped the idea, commenting: "It wasn't me. It was just fashion."[19] The constant factor is her singing voice: restrained, pure, clear, beautiful, and not using a lot of vibrato or melisma—early on she wailed passionately (e.g., "Drive"), but in a Bjork-like way rather than in an R'n'B fashion (although she clearly could sing this way if she wanted to). A general air of emotional reserve suffuses her lyrics: "I believe I might be having fun" ("Get Some Sleep"), which she glosses somewhat in interview: "I've only had fun in hindsight. My memories are quite fun, but at the time I was never having a good time"—a discourse of middle-class Kiwi understatement, with just a touch of artistic angst.[20]

---

[16] Bic Runga, *Live in Concert with the Christchurch Symphony,* Sony New Zealand 5148132000, 2003.

[17] An interesting comparison here would be the Split Enz/NZSO ENZSO project. ENZSO, *ENZSO,* Sony New Zealand 483870.9, 1996.

[18] Bic Runga, "Tour Posters," *bicRungadotnet,* 2004, http://www.bicrunga.net.nz/ tour_posters.htm.

[19] Ben Edwards, "Pop: Just Whistle a Happy Tune...," *The Sunday Times,* February 29, 2004, http://entertainment.timesonline.co.uk/tol/arts_and_entertainment/ article1029295.ece.

[20] Edwards, "Pop: Just Whistle a Happy Tune...."

On the subject of New Zealand: "You just can't be yourself at home,"
she says. "[In Paris] I can go to a club and just dance myself stupid . . .
things that I would just feel self-conscious doing in New Zealand."[21] But
this statement could be interpreted in a number of ways—the implication
that you can't "be yourself" in New Zealand continues the idea that there
is a "part" of her that isn't, and this could also be an ironic allusion to her
own ethnicity as Chinese-Māori. Keeping mum about ethnicity may also
be necessary for acceptance by mainstream white New Zealand—while we
might imagine that there could be nothing more Kiwi than being Māori, in
practice explicit statements about Māori identity tend to be interpreted by
the dominant group as challenges. However, Runga's façade of polite
reserve cracked when she told the *Belfast Telegraph*: "Did I grow up with
racism? Of course I did. I'm Māori Chinese," demonstrating perhaps the
difference between Runga's private views and her public persona.[22] But
this awareness of difference is also dramatised in her work. To be "Kiwi"
often means to keep to oneself, suppressing cultural histories and
differences in order to perpetuate a mythical unity, and the diversity of
Runga's strategies of self-presentation suggests that her "Kiwiness" is as
much a performance as her musical persona. She has a critical awareness
of the differences between herself and "Kiwis," between performer and
audience, a "double consciousness" which is common to performers and
marginalized ethnicities living as minorities in a society based on a myth
of sameness as unity.[23]

# References

Bannister, Matthew. "Kiwi Blokes: Recontextualising Pakeha Masculinities
    in a Global Setting." *Genders Online* 42 (2005),
    http://www.genders.org/g42/g42_bannister.html.
Butler, Judith. *Gender Trouble: Feminism and the Subversion of Identity.*
    New York: Routledge, 1990.

---

[21] Jo McCarroll, "The Next Bic Thing," *Sunday Star Times*, April 4, 2004,
http://www.bicrunga.net.nz/next_bic_thing.htm.
[22] John Meagher, "CD Music: Is this the Next Norah Jones?" *Belfast Telegraph*,
March 24, 2004, http://www.belfasttelegraph.co.uk/imported/cd-music-is-this-the-
next-norah-jones-13673077.html.
[23] Paul Gilroy, *The Black Atlantic: Modernity and Double Consciousness* (London,
New York: Verso, 1999), x.

Edwards, Ben. "Pop: Just Whistle a Happy Tune...." *The Sunday Times,* February 29, 2004, http://entertainment.timesonline.co.uk/tol/arts_ and_entertainment/article1029295.ece.

ENZSO. *ENZSO.* Sony 483870.9, 1996.

Felluga, Dino. "Modules on Marx: On Ideology." In *Introductory Guide to Critical Theory,* 2005, http://www.purdue.edu/guidetotheory/ marxism/modules/marxideology.html.

Gilroy, Paul. *The Black Atlantic: Modernity and Double Consciousness.* New York: Verso, 1999.

Green, Lucy. *Music, Gender, Education.* Cambridge: Cambridge University Press, 1997.

Huyssen, Andreas. "Mass Culture as Woman: Modernism's Other." In *Studies in Entertainment: Critical Approaches to Mass Culture,* edited by Tania Modleski, 188–207. Bloomington: Indiana University Press, 1986.

McCarroll, Jo. "The Next Bic Thing." *Sunday Star Times,* April 4, 2004, http://www.bicrunga.net.nz/next_bic_thing.htm.

Meagher, John. "CD Music: Is this the Next Norah Jones?" *Belfast Telegraph,* March 24, 2004, http://www.belfasttelegraph.co.uk/ imported/cd-music-is-this-the-next-norah-jones-13673077.html.

*Nature's Best.* Epic/Sony 5054952000, 2002.

Runga, Bic. "Get Some Sleep," *Youtube,* 2002, http://www.youtube.com/ watch?v=-C1yNyiUmF4.

—. "Listening for the Weather," *Youtube,* 2002, http://www.youtube.com/watch?v=LcqbtXSlcx8.

—. "Say After Me," *Youtube,* 2006, http://www.youtube.com/ watch?v=8WF2Js0Mc_s.

—. "Something Good," *Youtube,* 2002, http://www.youtube.com/ watch?v=UTRk4eXxwzA.

—. "Sway," *Youtube,* 1997, http://www.youtube.com/ watch?v=w28ZREQe3_Q.

—. "Tour Posters," *bicRungadotnet,* 2004, http://www.bicrunga.net.nz/ tour_posters.htm.

—. *Beautiful Collision.* Sony 5084039000, 2002.

—. *Birds.* Sony 82876755532, 2005.

—. *Drive.* Sony 488580.2, 1997.

—. *Live in Concert with the Christchurch Symphony.* Sony 5148132000, 2003.

Runga, Bic, Tim Finn, and Dave Dobbyn. *Together in Concert: Live.* CRA Records/Epic 5011402000, 2000.

Zuberi, Nabeel. "Sounds Like Us—Popular Music and Cultural Nationalism in Aotearoa/New Zealand." *Perfect Beat* 8, no. 3 (2007): 3–18.

CHAPTER NINE

"ANZAC, HOLLYWOOD, AND HOME":
CONSTRUCTING A NEW ZEALAND JAZZ
CULTURE

ALEISHA WARD

Gordon Mirams, in his 1945 study of New Zealanders and movie-going, stated: "If ever a national post-mortem is performed on us, I think there are three words written on New Zealand's heart—ANZAC, HOLLYWOOD, and HOME. But only a very rash prophet would venture to suggest which word will be carved the deepest."[1] Although Mirams was speaking of the influence of films on New Zealand culture, jazz in New Zealand could be described in a similar manner.

This paper examines the influence of Australian, American, and British cultures on jazz in New Zealand, the construction of a New Zealand jazz culture from the Jazz Age of the 1920s to the 1950s, and the establishment of rock'n'roll and the commercial recording industry in New Zealand. During this period, New Zealand jazz musicians responded to their country's changing relationships with Great Britain, the United States of America, and—to a lesser extent—Australia, by engaging and negotiating with the jazz cultures of those countries.

Jazz was one of the first global popular musics, developing at the dawn of the audio and visual technology era.[2] As gramophones and records, radio broadcasting, and film became accessible to the average person, so jazz spread rapidly throughout the western world. As with other genres of music developed during this period, the rapid spread of jazz also created

---

[1] Gordon Mirams, *Speaking Candidly: Films and People in New Zealand* (Hamilton: Paul's Book Arcade, 1945), 125.
[2] This is not referring to audiovisual technology, although commercial experiments were being made with synchronized sound and pictures from the early 1920s. The audiovisual era generally dates from the release of *The Jazz Singer* in 1927.

opportunities for jazz to be adapted to the local conditions of any given place or culture, before the tropes and ideologies of jazz, as it was conceived of in the United States, were set in stone in other countries or cultures.[3] Thus, jazz was a music that thrived and continues to thrive on being adopted into, and adapted to, other musical cultures.[4] It is possible that this type of dissemination and adaptation would not have happened at any other point in history, where the documents of jazz (in the forms of records and radio broadcasts) spread so far and so quickly, without the direct influence of human interaction as would occur with musicians presenting jazz in a live venue. In the case of jazz in New Zealand, this did not result in a syncretic (separate, regional) music, but rather a pastiche (defined as a work or culture formed from disparate sources) as New Zealand jazz musicians attempted to recreate American and/or British jazz.

During the early twentieth century, New Zealand was a small dominion at the edge of Britain's empire but, despite its size and relative isolation from England, it was not disconnected from the rest of the empire and the world. Through steam-powered travel and telecommunication technologies, New Zealand was connected not only to Great Britain, but also to Australia and the United States, among other countries. These technologies allowed people, cultural ideas, and consumer items to travel back and forth with increasing ease. One of the important effects that this trilogy of socio-economic links had on New Zealand was to create a cultural pastiche in which the artifacts of imported culture held the dominant position, but it is unclear which, if any, culture might be pre-eminent.[5]

---

[3] For examples of this, see the work of Catherine Parsonage and Hilary Moore on British jazz, Mike Heffley on European jazz cultures, and Andrew Bisset on Australian jazz: Catherine Parsonage, *The Evolution of Jazz in Britain, 1880–1935* (Burlington: Ashgate Publishing, 2005); Hilary Moore, *Inside British Jazz: Crossing Borders of Race, Nation and Class* (Aldershot: Ashgate Publishing, 2007); Mike Heffley, *Northern Sun, Southern Moon: Europe's Reinvention of Jazz* (New Haven: Yale University Press, 2005); Andrew Bisset, *Black Roots, White Flowers: A History of Jazz in Australia* (Sydney: ABC Enterprises, 1987).
[4] See, for instance, the work of Christopher Ballantine on jazz in South Africa: Christopher Ballantine, *Marabi Nights: Early South African Jazz and Vaudeville* (Johannesburg: Ravan Press, 1993).
[5] Miles Fairburn, "Is there a Good Case for New Zealand Exceptionalism?" in *Imagining New Zealand's Pasts*, ed. Tony Ballantyne and Brian Moloughney (Dunedin: Otago University Press, 2006), 146.

New Zealand was an enthusiastic importer of consumer items of all descriptions during the early and mid-twentieth century, and New Zealanders were eager to access the latest trends, fashions and technologies.[6] Through the importation of popular culture from Great Britain, Australia and the United States, New Zealanders were influenced by the sights, sounds, and speech patterns inherent in vaudeville, music hall, operetta, popular music, film, and other entertainments. Theatrical acts and companies from Great Britain, the United States, and Australia toured the combined New Zealand/Australia theatre circuits. Touring companies would often be presenting material that had been premiered in Europe, Great Britain and America in the previous one or two years.[7] The advent of films also had a significant impact on New Zealanders' exposure to foreign sights, sounds, and concepts, perhaps more so than other forms of entertainment, as films gave audiences more immediate insights into other cultures and ideas.[8]

The roles that each country played in New Zealand's psyche changed dramatically over the course of the first half of the twentieth century, and many of these changes were a result of international rather than domestic events. The end of World War I, the Great Depression, and World War II had far greater impacts on New Zealand than local events that occurred in response to these international events. Great Britain was at one extreme of these changes, as the cultural orientation and overt hegemony of New Zealand slowly shifted away from viewing Britain as "home" both culturally and politically. This shift was engendered by New Zealand's contact with other cultures and countries, particularly Australia and America, and could be seen across all aspects of New Zealand culture, from political ideas through to entertainment.[9] By the end of World War II, these shifting ideas meant that New Zealand was looking to the Pacific

---

[6] For further discussion on importation trends and access, see Peter Gibbons, "The Far Side of the Search for Identity: Reconsidering New Zealand History," *New Zealand Journal of History* 37, no. 1 (2003): 38–49.

[7] For example, J.C. Williamson Company staged the first legitimate production of Gilbert and Sullivan's *HMS Pinafore* in 1879–1880 (touring both Australia, and New Zealand), just eighteen months after its premiere in London, and at approximately the same time as the New York premiere. Michael Tallis and Joan Tallis, *The Silent Showman: Sir George Tallis, The Man Behind the World's Largest Entertainment Organisation of the 1920s* (Adelaide: Wakefield Press, 1999), 21.

[8] Nerida Elliot, "'Anzac, Hollywood and Home': Cinemas and Film-Going in Auckland 1909–1939" (M.A. diss., University of Auckland, 1989), 64–65.

[9] Gibbons, "The Far Side of the Search for Identity," 44.

region (particularly the United States of America) for cultural and political influences.

From 1920 through to the beginnings of the Pacific War in 1942, New Zealand viewed the United States of America as a convenient large-scale trading partner, one that was geographically closer than Great Britain.[10] The cultural influences that the trade relationship between New Zealand and the United States engendered appear to have been almost incidental, posing little interference to the hegemony of Great Britain. By the end of World War II, however, New Zealanders had begun to view the United States as a strong political and cultural power. This shift was due, in part, to the role that the United States' Expeditionary Forces played in the Pacific War and in New Zealand, as New Zealand was designated as a training, and rest and rehabilitation base.[11] It was also due to New Zealanders being enthusiastic importers of the products of the American entertainment industry.

Relations between New Zealand and Australia did not change as much as they did between New Zealand and the other two countries. The relationship between New Zealand and Australia was not one of political colonialism or hegemony; instead the relationship was analogous to that of siblings. Both were fairly young colonies of Great Britain, situated a long way from the motherland, with similar concerns regarding status and how they were viewed "back home."[12] Developments in the relationship between New Zealand and Australia also reflect the sibling analogy: as each country "grew" so did the relationship between them, becoming stronger and more enduring despite the differences between them.

The importation of jazz into New Zealand during the period under investigation reflected the changing relationships that New Zealand had with the United States, Great Britain, and Australia, and this is demonstrated through the use of media and negotiation of cultural agency. Jazz was imported into New Zealand through four different media and three countries. There was direct transmission from the United States, but jazz was also mediated and imported through Britain and Australia, and the jazz traditions forming in those two countries. The media of transmission ranged from the importation of sheet music and touring musicians through to radio broadcasts, records, and, after the advent of

---

[10] Keith Sinclair, *A History of New Zealand,* rev. ed. (Auckland: Penguin, 1991), 361–62.

[11] Denys Bevan, *United States Forces in New Zealand, 1942–1945* (Alexandra: Macpherson Publishing, 1992), 52, 94.

[12] James Belich, *Paradise Reforged: A History of New Zealanders from the 1880s to the Year 2000* (Auckland: Penguin Press, 2001), 51.

sound in films, soundtracks. This combination of mediation and types of media is very important to how a New Zealand jazz culture developed in the first half of the twentieth century. For the purposes of this paper, I will briefly examine recordings, sheet music, radio broadcasts, and touring musicians in relation to the process of cultural mediation in order to show how this negotiation affected the development of a New Zealand jazz culture.

Because jazz in New Zealand was included under the dance music banner for the first half of the twentieth century, its repertoire and performance practices were not specific to jazz music. This leads to a very broad definition of jazz: in the 1920s, jazz was any type of up-tempo dance music which could be "jazzed up" by arranging and performance techniques. It is only with the era of big band swing (mid-1930s) that jazz in New Zealand began to be associated with a particular set of musical tropes and repertoires.

For the majority of the period under investigation (until 1948), New Zealand did not have a commercial recording industry and had to rely on importations of records from Australia, Great Britain, and the United States. Importantly, for the development of a New Zealand jazz culture, this meant that—aside from listening to local musicians in a "live" situation—New Zealand musicians and fans during this period spent the majority of their time listening to imported recordings, the most of which were by British or American artists, with a smaller number of Australian groups. For musicians, their education would primarily focus on imitating these imports rather than emulating local musicians. This does not mean, however, that New Zealand musicians went unrecorded until this time. There is evidence that New Zealand musicians were recorded (either as sidemen or leaders) in Australia and in Great Britain, and their recordings were sold in New Zealand.[13] Within New Zealand, too, there were opportunities to record music privately; either through the recording booths at the larger music stores or on recording gramophones.[14]

Although sheet music was less important than recordings to the dissemination of jazz, globally, it was still very important to the importation of jazz into New Zealand, as it visually represented (to some degree) the rhythmic and harmonic practices that were involved in jazz, which could not always be identified aurally from recordings. Sheet music can be split into two broad categories, the first being standard piano/

---

[13] Laurie Lewis, *Arthur and the Nights at the Turntable: The Life and Times of a Jazz Broadcaster* (London: Excalibur Press, 1996), 94–95.
[14] Lewis Eady Ltd., "History," *Lewis Eady*, www.lewiseady.co.nz/history.html.

guitar/vocal arrangements sold in shops, the sort of music that the average fan might have bought if they were interested in learning to play jazz.[15] The second category comprises arrangements aimed at bandsmen and leaders. These arrangements were basic how-to orchestrations that were often part of a music trade magazine, or a newsletter such as *Melody Maker* or *Australian Musical News*. They could be used as written, or with a little embellishment, or they could form the basis of an arrangement by a musician, and tailored to a particular band.[16]

Radio broadcasting played an important role in the importation and adaptation of jazz in New Zealand, and falls into two categories: local New Zealand broadcasts, and broadcasts from Australia and the west coast of the United States which were accessed on shortwave radio. Dance music programmes were a staple of radio broadcasting in New Zealand from the earliest, privately run stations. From the 1920s through to the late 1940s, popular modern dance music was based, in some measure, on some form of jazz: in the early years ragtime and the dixieland styles were the progenitors of much dance music, and, from the mid-1930s, there was the big band/swing craze. Although it was not until 1940 that there was a regular jazz programme on New Zealand radio (in the form of *Rhythm on Record*), jazz was a staple of the modern dance music programmes and *Make Believe Ballroom* formats.[17] These programmes mostly used records imported from Great Britain or North America, but would also broadcast relays from local cabarets.[18]

In the 1920s and 1930s there were strict limits on what could be played and when, with the Radio Broadcasting Company of New Zealand (RBC) (later the New Zealand Broadcasting Board [NZBB]) issuing detailed skeleton programmes to stations each week. These skeleton programmes outlined what type of material could be presented and what time(s) it was acceptable to present it. One reason for these limitations was a matter of coordination between stations, so that different stations were not playing the same material at the same time. Another reason was that the broadcasting officials of the day believed that the listening public needed

---

[15] Dennis O. Huggard, ed., *Desmond 'Spike' Donovan, Thoughts of a Musician* (Auckland: Dennis Huggard, 1998), 6.

[16] See, for example, *Australian Music-Maker and Dance Band News*, March, 1936.

[17] Lewis, *Arthur and the Nights at the Turntable*, 85–89.

[18] See, for example, programming for 3YA, Christchurch, in *The New Zealand Radio Record and Electric Home Journal*, December 20, 1928. Published by the Radio Broadcasting Company of New Zealand.

to be educated, not entertained.[19] In the case of jazz, the limitations related to time of day and type. Jazz was not supposed to be played before 8pm (and played mostly after 9pm), and sweet or symphonic jazz (in the style of Paul Whiteman) was favoured over hot jazz (played by bands such as King Oliver's Creole Band).[20] Even the day of the week appears to have had an impact on whether jazz was played or not, with jazz featured in dance programmes on Friday and Saturday nights more than on any other day.[21] The only exceptions to these regulations were the relay broadcasts from cabarets, as the RBC/NZBB had no control over (and often did not know) what material was presented. These restrictions were eased in the 1940s, but there were still limits on what jazz could be played when.[22]

Little has been written about which international stations New Zealanders could access via shortwave radio. It is known, however, that listeners with appropriate equipment were able to pick up broadcasts from Australia (mostly those from Sydney, Melbourne, and Perth) if they were on the west coast of New Zealand, and from the western states of America (as far inland as Colorado) if they were on the east coast of New Zealand.[23] Early New Zealand jazz pioneer Epi Shalfoon recalled in interviews that he first heard American jazz broadcasts on his shortwave radio set as a teenager in Opotiki, and that these broadcasts fired his interest in jazz.[24] Although there is little evidence at this point, the possibility that incipient jazz musicians were accessing jazz from Australia or the United States has the potential to be very important in constructing an understanding of how jazz in New Zealand developed the way that it did.

Touring musicians appear to have played a smaller role than recordings and broadcasts in influencing jazz musicians in New Zealand. Few jazz bands toured within the vaudeville circuit, and the number decreased as vaudeville suffered under the rise of movies. Still fewer appear to have toured New Zealand outside the circuits, but those groups that did tour— such as the Savoy Havana Band (also known as Bert Ralton and His

---

[19] Patrick Day, *The Radio Years: A History of Broadcasting in New Zealand.* Vol. 1 (Auckland: Auckland University Press, 1994), 86–87, 168–69.
[20] For definitions of sweet, symphonic, and hot jazz, see "Jazz," *New Grove Dictionary of Jazz*, 2nd ed., Vol. 2 (New York: Grove Dictionaries, 2002), 361-69.
[21] See, for example, NZRR, various schedules for 1929 and 1931.
[22] See, for example, *New Zealand Listener* (1944).
[23] Day, *The Radio Years*, 104.
[24] Reo Sheirtcliff, "Dancing in the Dark: A Memoir of Epi Shalfoon," *Music in New Zealand* 10 (1990): 41; "High-Powered American Stations," *New Zealand Radio Record and Electric Home Journal*, December 20, 1929, 27.

World Famous Savoy Havana Band) in 1924, Sammy Lee and his Americanadians in 1940, or Artie Shaw and The Neptuners (officially U.S. Navy Band #501) in 1943—appear to have had a great impact on jazz musicians in New Zealand.[25] The effects that touring musicians had on jazz in New Zealand ranged from arranging styles through to performance, technical, and stylistic practices. Particularly noted by New Zealand jazz musicians was the method of projection (or, in the jazz vernacular, blowing), which helped to fill in the one major aspect of jazz that they could not perceive from recordings. New Zealand musicians were also very impressed by the stagecraft and style of these touring bands, as they presented themselves as artists and entertainers, rather than the near-invisible providers of dance music.[26]

The notion of cultural pastiche is embodied in the construction of a New Zealand jazz culture. It has been demonstrated that jazz was imported into New Zealand directly from the United States and also mediated through the jazz cultures developing in Great Britain and Australia. This mediation of American jazz through British and Australian jazz traditions means that by the time jazz was imported into New Zealand it had multiple, layered influences, but these influences were decontextualized from their original sources. Not only was jazz in New Zealand decontextualized from the original American jazz culture, it was also, to a lesser extent, decontextualized from the British and Australian jazz cultures. Jazz historian John Whiteoak describes this situation as being one of loss and mutation of the original culture but, while it can certainly be described as such, it could also be described as a pastiche, providing the base for a new culture.[27]

Aspects of New Zealand culture developed out of a pastiche of British, American, and Australian cultures during this period, and so it is for the jazz culture of New Zealand. The decontextualization and transformation of jazz through America, Britain, and Australia was a major factor in how jazz was adopted into New Zealand society, and in the development of a New Zealand jazz culture. This trio pastiche of American, British, and

---

[25] Savoy Havana Band: "Super-Vaudeville Programme," *J.C. Williamson*, His Majesty's Theatre, Auckland, December 6, 1924; Sammy Lee and his Americanadians: "The New Metropole," *New Zealand Herald*, May 6, 1940; Artie Shaw and the Neptuners: "Americans Gesture—Dance for New Zealanders," *New Zealand Herald*, August 7, 1943.

[26] Dale Alderton, interview by author, September 10, 2002; and Johnny Williams, interview by author, April 15, 2003.

[27] John Whiteoak, "Introduction," *Playing Ad Lib: Improvisatory Music in Australia 1836–1970* (Sydney: Currency Press, 1999), xiii–xiv.

Australian cultures formed the basis of how jazz was perceived in New Zealand society, and how it was transformed into a music culture that, while it retained its links to the jazz traditions of America (and also of Britain and Australia), began to take on a New Zealand identity.

# References

"Americans Gesture—Dance for New Zealanders." *New Zealand Herald*, August 7, 1943.

*Australian Music-Maker and Dance Band News*. March, 1936.

Ballantine, Christopher. *Marabi Nights: Early South African Jazz and Vaudeville*. Johannesburg: Ravan Press, 1993.

Belich, James. *Paradise Reforged: A History of New Zealanders from the 1880s to the Year 2000*. Auckland: Penguin Press, 2001.

Bevan, Denys. *United States Forces in New Zealand, 1942–1945*. Alexandra: Macpherson Publishing, 1992.

Bisset, Andrew. *Black Roots, White Flowers: A History of Jazz in Australia*. Sydney: ABC Enterprises, 1987.

Day, Patrick. *The Radio Years: A History of Broadcasting in New Zealand*. Vol. 1. Auckland: Auckland University Press, 1994.

Elliott, Nerida. "'Anzac, Hollywood and Home': Cinemas and Film-Going in Auckland 1909–1939." M.A. diss., University of Auckland, 1989.

Fairburn, Miles. "Is There a Good Case for New Zealand Exceptionalism?" In *Disputed Histories: Imagining New Zealand's Pasts*, edited by Tony Ballantyne and Brian Moloughney, 143–67. Dunedin: Otago University Press, 2006.

Gibbons, Peter. "The Far Side of the Search for Identity: Reconsidering New Zealand History." *New Zealand Journal of History* 37, no. 1 (2003): 38–49.

Heffley, Mike. *Northern Sun, Southern Moon: Europe's Reinvention of Jazz*. New Haven: Yale University Press, 2005.

"High-Powered American Stations." *The New Zealand Radio Record and Electric Home Journal*. December 20, 1929, 27.

Huggard, Dennis O., ed. *Desmond 'Spike' Donovan, Thoughts of a Musician*. Auckland: Dennis Huggard, 1998.

Lewis Eady Ltd. "History." *Lewis Eady*. www.lewiseady.co.nz/history.html.

Lewis, Laurie. *Arthur and the Nights at the Turntable: The Life and Times of a Jazz Broadcaster*. London: Excalibur Press, 1996.

*Melody Maker*. London: IPC.

Mirams, Gordon. *Speaking Candidly: Films and People in New Zealand*.

Hamilton: Paul's Book Arcade, 1945.

Moore, Hilary. *Inside British Jazz: Crossing Borders of Race, Nation and Class.* Aldershot: Ashgate Publishing, 2007.

*New Grove Dictionary of Jazz*, 2nd ed. 3 vols. New York: Grove Dictionaries, 2002.

*New Zealand Listener.* Wellington: New Zealand Broadcasting Corporation, 1944.

*New Zealand Radio Record and Electric Home Journal, The.* December 20, 1928.

Parsonage, Catherine. *The Evolution of Jazz in Britain, 1880–1935.* Burlington: Ashgate Publishing, 2005.

Sheirtcliff, Reo. "Dancing in the Dark: A Memoir of Epi Shalfoon." *Music in New Zealand* 10 (1990): 40–45.

Sinclair, Keith. *A History of New Zealand,* rev. ed. Auckland: Penguin Press, 1991.

"Super-Vaudeville Programme." *J.C. Williamson.* His Majesty's Theatre, Auckland, December 6, 1924.

Tallis, Michael, and Joan Tallis. *The Silent Showman: Sir George Tallis, The Man Behind the World's Largest Entertainment Organisation of the 1920s.* Adelaide: Wakefield Press, 1999.

"The New Metropole," *New Zealand Herald.* May 6, 1940.

Whiteoak, John. *Playing Ad Lib: Improvisatory Music in Australia 1836–1970.* Sydney: Currency Press, 1999.

# CHAPTER TEN

# MIKE NOCK:
# A NEW ZEALAND VOICE IN JAZZ

# NORMAN MEEHAN

*Mike Nock Solo*, released in New Zealand and Australia in 1980, possesses a "New Zealand" quality; it sounds somehow as though it was made in, and is of New Zealand. Nock was aware of this quality, and remarked: "Interestingly enough that album served as a solace to some New Zealanders I knew who were going through a difficult time while living overseas, so maybe there was something there that resonated with them."[1] This paper discusses the ways Nock's music evokes New Zealand by considering the landscapes—both physical and cultural—from which it arose.

## The Cultural Landscape

As a child in Ngaruawahia, Nock formed a band with other children in the neighborhood:

> We had a piano, a cornet, a guitar, together with some miscellaneous noisemakers—such as alarm clocks—anything we could make a sound with. Spike Jones and his City Slickers were an early influence; we'd heard them on the radio. Of course we couldn't play any tunes as such, so we made up our own. It was a case of improvisational necessity being the mother of composition.[2]

---

[1] All unattributed quotes are drawn from interviews the author conducted with Mike Nock between 2004 and 2009.
[2] Alwyn Lewis and Laurie Lewis, "Mike Nock Interview," *Cadence*, July (1992): 12.

This "do-it-yourself" (DIY) approach was indicative of the economically straightened circumstances of a rural community in the 1940s, but was also a reflection of a common New Zealand attitude; one of jumping in with what you have and making do. It was partly a function of the country's geographical isolation and lack of equipment, and partly a reflection of the "pioneering spirit" of the place. Nock believed that "can do" attitude translated into considerable cultural energy: "The New Zealand I grew up in was very much a 'do-it-yourself' culture, when people hadn't forgotten the hardships of the depression and wartime rationing. It was like a throwback to an earlier, more self-sufficient time. People were always ready to give things a go."

This DIY attitude had two positive consequences for Nock: a willingness to boldly try things, even if he didn't know too much about them; and a willingness to use whatever resources were to hand to make music. Art historian Gregory O'Brien commented on this, reporting that Nock has said there is a "New Zealand" way of going about music: "Probably a provincial cast of mind—which is about stitching it together, makeshift, sometimes compelling but also, as you might guess, limited."[3] While Nock had almost no technical training as a young pianist, by working hard over the years he has overcome those limitations. Nevertheless, his playing and his music retain something of that makeshift spirit.

In terms of self-confidence, the benefits of this DIY culture are obvious. A more subtle value that crept into Nock's art because of the DIY culture was a willingness to use whatever materials were to hand to make his music. Nock uses techniques from many styles to forge his music, and his catalogue is consequently very diverse.[4] New Zealand art critic Hamish Keith commented on this value more generally:

> New Zealand from its very beginning has had a rich history of adoption and adaptation of the things the original travellers carried here with them and the things subsequent travellers brought. If we deserve a reputation for ingenuity and inventiveness, the reason lies there and not in some miracle of number-eight fencing wire.[5]

Nock has consistently cobbled his music together with bits and pieces from all over the place. As a New Zealander he is not alone in this

---

[3] Gregory O'Brien, e-mail message to author, March 22, 2009.
[4] Nock's recordings include music for solo jazz and classical piano, small and large jazz bands, choir, string quartet, and chamber and symphony orchestra.
[5] Hamish Keith, *Native Wit* (Auckland: Random House, 2008), 132.

approach. James Belich wrote: "Much Pākehā folk culture seems to belong to someone else, notably our four big others: Old Britons, Australians, Americans and, last but not least, Māori."[6] Nock's music, which some writers have suggested is evocative of New Zealand, is like this; it's drawn from many sources. A brief survey of some of his recordings from the last thirty years reveals his appropriation of: tangos ("Tango for Gretchen Rodriguez," 1990), sambas ("Song of Brazil," 1979), music derived from western art music sources ("Variations on Pachelbel's Canon," 1994), "world music" values ("Dance of the Global Village," 1990), and many others.

At a music forum in 2009, New Zealand composer Ross Harris said that he had always told his students that the thing that marks New Zealand music as singular is that New Zealand composers are free to do anything; lacking the historical burdens of composers from other countries, they can do—and use—anything they want to.

In light of this, it's unsurprising that for many New Zealanders, Tourism New Zealand's promotion of this county as "100% Pure" struck "a jarring note."[7] That was because much of New Zealand's contemporary culture (like most New Zealanders) comes from all over the place. New Zealand culture is not pure; it's assembled from those various pieces to make something unique. The nature of the constituent parts themselves is not important, it is how they are put together that is most meaningful. In terms of Nock's music (and that of others with a similar aesthetic), this could be described as a postmodern approach. That's reasonable, but what gives it a specifically New Zealand flavour? Hamish Keith has suggested:

> 'Nationalism in art,' [Bryan Robertson] said, 'is just another form of militant provincialism. National characteristics, on the other hand, need to be recognised and cherished.' … Art belongs to a place and people not so much by what it says, although that is sometimes the case, as by how it is said.[8]

Nock has been catholic in the musical resources he's appropriated, borrowing harmonic games, sounds and rhythms from other musics. While eclecticism is not a uniquely New Zealand characteristic, Nock has a New Zealand way of assembling his music, which distinguishes it from other

---

[6] James Belich, *Paradise Reforged: A History of the New Zealanders from the 1880s to the Year 2000* (Auckland: The Penguin Press, 2001), 346.
[7] John McCrone, "The Flight of the Kiwi," *Dominion Post*, September 13, 2008, Your Weekend.
[8] Keith, *Native Wit*, 165.

postmodern music in jazz. Why? Because Nock's music and career has been informed by his *cultural* heritage as a New Zealander:

> One of the big drawbacks of New Zealand culture is the 'tall poppy syndrome,' as it is in Australia. When I grew up in New Zealand, one of the worst things you could be was a 'skite.' You couldn't stand above the crowd. You had to merge in all the time. I've spoken to many people my age from New Zealand and this is definitely one of the things that affected us, and it made us self-conscious. Self-consciousness is damaging to self-expression. I see a lot of self-consciousness in New Zealand art; I see it in movies for example. Obviously it's getting better, but it is one of the things we have to deal with.

It was this very "New Zealand" value—the Tall Poppy Syndrome, self-consciousness—that led Nock to leave New Zealand when he was only eighteen. And yet its attendant modesty is a personal value that he has retained and that has influenced his career and his music.

New Zealand group The Flight of the Conchords has turned this self-effacing tendency into a virtue. On their website they describe themselves as "Formerly New Zealand's fourth most popular guitar-based comedy folk duo" and their light-hearted self-mockery has been significant in their conquest of the US airwaves.[9]

For Nock, the music itself provides evidence of this self-effacing tendency. *Ondas*, *Strata*, and parts of *Mike Nock Solo*—compositionally at least—are albums that feature minimal resources crafted carefully to make the most of the spare materials in play. And on these albums his piano playing is also frequently stripped back; there is a bare bones quality to the music that is part of its appeal.

But there's something more here too. Much jazz that could be described as postmodern is also ironic, and often parodic. And it often seems that jazz musicians writing and playing this way quote from their sources with a "knowing wink."[10] I asked Nock about his musical philosophy and he denied any allegiance to postmodernism, instead emphasizing the emotional value of his music:

> No one really cares if you are the greatest or the cleverest or the hippest; generally, the punters want to get something . . . I like to give people an experience that may prove in some way uplifting, a 'positive something.' I want it to have an effect in the world—music is an emotional communication and to me that's the most important thing.

---

[9] Flight of the Conchords, *Flight of the Conchords*, http://www.conchords.co.nz.
[10] Jazz pianists Uri Caine, Ethan Iverson, and Vijay Iyer, for example.

This attitude means that Nock's borrowing from so many sources is guileless—it's done to serve the emotional values of his music—and is not a comment on the provenance of his materials. And the lack of irony and artifice give the music directness and honesty that is unusual.

## The Physical Landscape

When asked if there were formal or technical aspects of his music that made it sound like it was from or of New Zealand, Nock said:

> I don't think so. The one *material* thing I've always felt that has influence on my music, is the New Zealand landscape . . . It's hard to pinpoint specific things, but water and the greenery are important . . . I love the thought of writing slow music that really reflects the landscape, those rolling hills that just go on and on. It's difficult to do that in a jazz context, although maybe *Ondas* touches on that in some ways.[11]

New Zealand composer Douglas Lilburn discussed the centrality of the landscape to the creation of an authentic New Zealand music, and that idea seems to inhabit Nock's recordings, particularly those from the late 1970s and early 1980s. Richard Nunns, in his liner notes to Nock's *Strata* album (1984), suggested: "The material included here has something to do with coming home (Nock lives in New Jersey but returns to New Zealand regularly); has something to do with capturing an antipodean facet of Nock's musical vision."[12]

As a musician and a close friend of Nock, Nunns was in an excellent position to comment on the characteristics of Nock's music which owed a debt to his New Zealand origins. It's a side of the music that Nock is himself aware of: "[Nock] talks of the effect on him of the New Zealand landscape where there was always water to be seen. The result is that his own compositions contain what he calls 'the flowingness of water.'"[13] And the pieces do flow. In writing music that evokes those "slow rolling

---

[11] Norman Meehan, "Mike Nock on New Zealand Jazz," in *Jazz Aotearoa*, ed. Richard Hardie and Allan Thomas (Wellington: Steele Roberts, 2009), 61. Nock recorded *Ondas* for ECM in 1981, having lived most of the previous twenty years in the United States, and yet, in some ways, it is the record that is most redolent of his homeland. Landscape is arguably one of the keys here.

[12] Richard Nunns, "Liner Notes," to Mike Nock, *Strata*, Kiwi/Pacific SLC 179, 1984.

[13] Dennis Pryor, "Television," *The Age,* October 27, 1994, Arts Section.

hills that just go on and on" and "the flowingness of water," Nock has
invested his music with something uniquely his in the jazz world.

If, as Nock suggests, it is not the musical devices that locate the music
here, but rather some kind of "evocation of place" that achieves this effect,
how does that work? Hamish Keith has suggested that: "It is the
experience of landscape, not its appearance, which provides the cultural
grid, which gives our imagination a place to anchor."[14] New Zealand has a
landscape that can sometimes overawe us. And as a modest people—
humility is a national trait—New Zealanders' experience of their
landscape may be related to that.[15] Standing on a glacier or driving
through the McKenzie Basin, one can feel like small and alone: an actor
on a very big set.

Specifically it is the hypnotic affect of the rippling *arpeggios* and
relentless *ostinati*, the sparse melodic and harmonic material, and the
acoustic space of the records that evoke this impression. The New Zealand
landscape can be experienced as subtle variations on a theme (those "slow
rolling hills that just go on and on"): we often move slowly relative to the
land. In this music, the impression of movement is found in the *ostinati*
and arpeggiated figures that form the ground, and the subtle, slowly
changing melodies might be said to give an impression of the slowly
changing details of the landscape. It's cinematic in this way.

On *Ondas* in particular, that impression is further enhanced by the
acoustic space of the recording—very reverberant and evocative of wide-
open spaces. This is sometimes referred to as the "Nordic sound" of ECM
recordings, but it's a sonic value that could equally well be applied to this
country and to the way the landscape here can make us feel small and
alone. ECM owner Manfred Eicher, discussing what he sought when he
made records, said: "The crucial thing is for a tone or mood to be
created—an atmosphere that sincerely expresses what one wishes to
convey of oneself and one's emotions. Music is the art that speaks directly
to the soul."[16] In the case of *Ondas*, it is also an art that speaks directly
from Nock's soul as a New Zealander. And what he says reminds us of our
experience of being from this place with its misty backblocks and
windswept beaches.

Exactly how this works is mysterious, but somehow this music has
associations for many listeners. In many cases, listeners familiar with the
New Zealand landscape find the images and sensations evoked by the

---

[14] Keith, *Native Wit*, 37.
[15] McCrone, "The Flight of the Kiwi," 8–11.
[16] Paul Griffiths and Steve Lake, *Horizons Touched* (London: Granta, 2007), 10.

music easy to associate with New Zealand's land and sky. It's a value not lost to reviewers: "In the rich texture of ["Aurora Australis"] and other tracks there is a nostalgic edge, a feeling for New Zealand, his home country."[17]

## The Perception of Nock as a New Zealand Artist

Any encounter with art is a two-way street and the perceptions of the viewer are an essential ingredient in the mix. Which is not, I hasten to say, an argument for the dumb idea that a work of art is only what we think it is. It is what the artist intended and what we in our turn make of that.[18]

Many New Zealanders know Nock is from here, and when New Zealanders listen to "Land of the Long White Cloud" or "Oparara" or "Bush Walk," they hear something of their homeland. A seed is planted by the knowledge that Nock is from here, or by a title that evokes New Zealand, and that conditions their response: they "hear" New Zealand in the music. The musical devices Nock uses—ones that create the impression of space or the "flowingness of water"—re-affirm that association. However, someone from the mid-west of the United States or Canada or coastal Australia could equally well hear their homeland evoked by the same tracks.

But when we marry that evocative aspect of the music to its eclecticism—without irony—and the rough and ready aspect of some of it, we get closer to something that might be described as a New Zealand sound. If Nock has a specifically "New Zealand" voice in jazz, perhaps it has something to do with these values.

Is New Zealand music identifiable solely on the basis of how it sounds? That's very unlikely. However, what is more important is that musicians and composers strive for their "own" sound, and in doing so perhaps something of their origins may emerge in the music. Nock has certainly succeeded in that endeavour.

---

[17] Mark Bazeley, "Mike Nock: Strata," *Jazz*, Summer/Autumn (1986): 58.
[18] Keith, *Native Wit*, 175.

# References

Bazeley, Mark. "Mike Nock: Strata." *Jazz*, Summer/Autumn (1986): 58.
Belich, James. *Paradise Reforged: A History of the New Zealanders from the 1880s to the Year 2000*. Auckland: The Penguin Press, 2001.
Flight of the Conchords, *Flight of the Conchords*. http://www.conchords.co.nz.
Griffiths, Paul, and Steve Lake. *Horizons Touched*. London: Granta, 2007.
Keith, Hamish. *Native Wit*. Auckland: Random House, 2008.
Lealand, Geoff. *A Foreign Egg in Our Nest? American Popular Culture in New Zealand*. Wellington: Victoria University Press, 1988.
Lewis, Alwyn, and Laurie Lewis. "Mike Nock Interview." *Cadence*, July (1992): 14–20.
McCrone, John. "The Flight of the Kiwi." *The Dominion Post*, September 13, 2008, Your Weekend.
Meehan, Norman. "Mike Nock on New Zealand and Jazz." In *Jazz Aotearoa*, edited by Richard Hardie and Allan Thomas, 56–68. Wellington: Steele Roberts, 2009.
Nock, Mike. *Climbing*. Tomato 2696502, 1979.
—. *Dark and Curious*. ABC 846 873–2, 1990.
—. *Everybody Wants to Go to Heaven*. Naxos/Jazz 86073, 2000.
—. *Mike Nock Solo*. Ode SODE 121, 1978.
—. *Ondas*. ECM 1220 829 161–2, 1981.
—. *Strata*. Kiwi/Pacific SLC 179,1984.
—. *Succubus*. Sutra SUS 1005, 1980.
—. *Touch*. Birdland BL001, 1994.
Nunns, Richard. "Liner Notes." Mike Nock, *Strata*. Kiwi/Pacific SLC 179, 1984.
Pryor, Dennis. "Television." *The Age*, October 27, 1994, Arts Section.

CHAPTER ELEVEN

NEW ZEALAND IDENTITY IN POPULAR MUSIC:
VOWEL DIFFERENCES
BETWEEN SINGING AND SPEAKING

ANDY GIBSON

## Prior Research on Pronunciation in Singing

It has been well established that when people sing, they use different pronunciation than when they speak. The seminal study by Trudgill analyzed a number of pronunciation features in records by *The Beatles*, *The Rolling Stones*, and other British artists.[1] He found high rates of American pronunciation features.[2] Trudgill's explanation for the use of these features was that British singers were modifying their linguistic behaviour in the direction of a model group with whom they wished to identify. In this case, the model group was American singers, who had been a dominant cultural force throughout much of the history of recorded popular music. In music dating from the mid-1960s onwards, Trudgill found that the usage of American features decreased to some extent. This decrease was considered to be the result of the fast-increasing success of British bands and a concurrent decrease in the cultural dominance of America. Trudgill's analysis of punk bands *The Clash* and *Sham '69* found that their singing exhibited pronunciation features associated with working-class British youth, however a number of American accent features continued to be used. Trudgill explains this mixture as representing

---

[1] Peter Trudgill, *On Dialect: Social and Geographical Perspectives* (Oxford: Blackwell, 1983).

[2] Seeing as there are many dialects of English in the United States, the term "American" is used as a loose description for a range of pronunciation features which are associated with American accents, though the convention in singing may be biased towards Southern varieties and African-American Vernacular English.

the singers' desire to identify with both the dominant American model and with an authentic local identity.

In New Zealand, sociolinguistic research on the sung accents of a range of artists found that even singers who claimed they did not want to sound American still used many American features.[3] Several singers also claimed that it was difficult to sing in a New Zealand accent.[4] Similar to the punk bands mentioned above, these artists ended up with a mixture of local features and American features. These results raise several questions about pronunciation shifts between singing and speaking. Why do people shift towards an American accent when singing? Are they shifting towards a group they wish to identify with? If this is the case, why can't singers completely shift their accent to a local variety even when they wish to do so? Either the desire to identify with the American model is strong and subconscious, or there is some other mechanism at work.

## Alternative Explanation for Differences between Singing and Speech

Trudgill briefly raised the argument that pronunciation shifts in singing may be explained by the sociolinguistic notion of "appropriateness," the fact that certain speech styles are appropriate to some contexts and not others. It is appropriate to sing in an American accent because this is the accent most frequently used in the context of popular music. As an example, Trudgill states that "the singing of pop music in this way ... is no different from vicars preaching in the register appropriate to Church of England sermons."[5] Trudgill abandoned this argument, however, on the grounds that appropriateness "is not enough on its own to provide an explanation for why it is this type of singing which is regulated in this way, nor why it is characterized by this set of pronunciation rules and tendencies rather than some other."[6]

In order to provide the kind of detailed explanations which the notion of appropriateness alone cannot provide, a model which emphasises the importance of memory in language processing is needed. Recent developments in exemplar theories of language perception and production

---

[3] Anna Coddington, "Singing as We Speak? An Exploratory Investigation of Singing Pronunciation in New Zealand Popular Music" (M.A. diss., University of Auckland, 2004).

[4] Coddington, "Singing as We Speak?" 71.

[5] Trudgill, *On Dialect*, 143.

[6] Ibid., 143–44.

may provide a useful framework for understanding how exposure affects pronunciation in singing, as well as in speech.[7] Exemplar theories of language processing claim that language events are stored in memory with acoustic detail, and are also indexed with social and contextual information. Under an exemplar account, context-dependent appropriateness would be driven by the co-occurrence of certain pronunciation styles with certain speakers or contexts.

A New Zealander is born into a world of popular culture and encounters a multitude of artists singing in American accents, but only a minority of counter-examples. Having heard popular music sung in a certain way the majority of the time, and indeed singing along with it, New Zealanders then tend to write and sing their own songs with similar pronunciation. Seeing as singing is contextually different from speaking on just about all levels, exemplar theories would predict that it may have a very different set of pronunciation norms. If a person receives consistent exposure to a certain set of vowel sounds in a well-defined context, it will seem natural to produce these same vowel sounds when producing language in that context.

Even if exposure is the primary driver behind accent shifts in singing, it is still necessary to account for those acts of identity when people really do wish to identify with a certain group, and do so by modifying their linguistic behaviour. Why do some people act against their conditioning and sing in an accent more similar to their own speaking accent? There are many examples of singers using features from their spoken accent in song. I have already mentioned punk bands such as *The Clash*, who used a mixture of vernacular British and American pronunciation features. A more recent study has found this same kind of mixing of local and American features in Britpop band *Oasis* in the 1990s.[8] Another documented occurrence of this is in Australian hip hop, where rappers mainly use Australian variants of vowels;[9] differing from popular rap artists in New Zealand, whose pronunciation, of at least the "r" variable,

---

[7] For an overview of exemplar theories of language, see Janet Pierrehumbert, "The Next Toolkit," *Journal of Phonetics* 34, no. 4 (2006): 516–30.

[8] Carl Johan Carlsson, "The Way They Sing It: Englishness and Pronunciation in English Pop and Rock," *Moderna Språk* 95, no. 2 (2001): 161; Paul Simpson, "Language, Culture and Identity: With (Another) Look at Accents in Pop and Rock Singing," *Multilingua* 18, no. 4 (1999): 343–67.

[9] Renae O'Hanlon, "Australian Hip Hop: A Sociolinguistic Investigation," *Australian Journal of Linguistics* 26, no. 2 (2006): 193–209.

follows the American hip hop model.[10] It is in these counter-examples to American-accented singing where the explanation initially proposed by Trudgill becomes more directly relevant, with pronunciation style reflecting the singer's desire to be associated with a certain group. In these instances, the effects of identity construction may outweigh the effects of linguistic conditioning. When singers become aware of a certain American feature in their singing, they may ask themselves what it means. They may attribute it simply to sounding appropriate to the context, or they may conclude that American-accented singing connotes an American identity. In the latter case, they may respond by making a conscious effort to sing with pronunciation more similar to their speech.

In order to test the questions presented above, the differences between singing and speech first need to be adequately described and quantified. The results below provide a first step in that direction.

## Comparison of Singing and Speech

I have analyzed the pronunciation of three semi-professional New Zealand singers, all of whom are Pākehā males in their early 30s who write their own music. Dylan Storey plays alternative rock/blues, Andrew Keoghan is a singer/songwriter who usually performs as a solo artist, and John Guy Howell sings in the *Broken Heartbreakers*, which is an indie/folk band. For each artist, I obtained a vocal take from a recording of one or more songs, and then recorded them reciting the lyrics to those songs. This allowed direct comparison of pronunciation between the sung and spoken contexts, while holding other linguistic factors constant. To provide contextual information to supplement these recordings, the artists were interviewed about their music and about their singing pronunciation.

To illustrate a few of the differences which occur between singing and speaking, I will provide a short analysis of a line from Andrew Keoghan's song "Gloria":

"There's something in the way her hair hangs."

A range of pronunciation differences between the sung and spoken recordings are immediately apparent. For example, there is an "r" sound at the end of the words "her" and "hair" in singing, where no "r" sound is produced in the spoken version. Another salient difference is the

---

[10] Andy Gibson, "Non-Prevocalic /r/ in New Zealand Hip-Hop," *New Zealand English Journal* 19 (2005): 5–12.

alternation between "something" with an "ng" sound at the end in the spoken version, and "somethin'" with "n" at the end, in singing. One striking example of a difference in vowel pronunciation is found when comparing the sung and spoken versions of the word "hair." A notable feature of New Zealand English is that the vowels in the words "ear" and "air" have merged together so that the underlined words in the phrase "here is my hair" sound the same for many speakers. When Andrew is reciting the song, the word "hair" sounds something like "here." However, in singing, the vowels unmerge, with Andrew using a vowel in "hair" which most likely does not exist in his speech at all. In order to quantify some of the differences between singing and speech, I have conducted an acoustic analysis of a range of vowels. To provide some context for the more detailed results which follow, it is important to first establish how the singers responded to the interview questions about their singing pronunciation.

## Interview Responses

Dylan seems highly conscious of the accent he uses when he sings. He says that there is a tension between not wanting to sound American, and finding it difficult to use New Zealand vowels in singing. He states that it is "painful to blatantly sing American vowels, but going the other way is quite difficult too . . . it does seem easier to sing an American accent." Andrew says that when singing the song under analysis, he "gave it more edge than my natural voice . . . it's definitely not completely natural." He appears to be aware that there is a difference between singing and speaking, but does not seem concerned about whether or not this difference results in the projection of an American identity. John, like Dylan, is overtly aware of his singing accent. He is the only one of the three singers, however, who says that he has "become aware of it and actually made a conscious decision to sing more in my speaking voice."

This range of stances between the three singers gives us a good opportunity to assess some of the questions raised in the first sections of the paper. It is of interest to determine not only whether the singers' speech and singing differ, but also whether their pronunciation data aligns with the sentiments expressed in the interview. Of particular interest is the extent to which John is successful in his effort to sing with his spoken accent.

## Acoustic Analysis of Vowels

My analysis consists of measurements of the pronunciation of eight different vowels across the sung and spoken contexts. It is outside the scope of this paper to present all of this data, so I will focus on the results for just two of these vowels; the DRESS vowel and the TRAP vowel.[11] Pronunciation is measured using spectrograms, which visually represent a sound's frequency and amplitude over time. Measurements of the first two formant frequencies of a vowel can describe the position of the tongue in the mouth. Both DRESS and TRAP are notably raised in New Zealand English, compared to most other varieties of English, meaning that the tongue is relatively close to the roof of the mouth for the pronunciation of these vowels.[12] The American pronunciation of the vowels would have a lower tongue position than spoken New Zealand English. Given the interview responses above, we would expect a lower (more American) tongue position in singing than speech for both Dylan and Andrew. If John is successful in his desire to sing in his spoken accent, we would expect the tongue position to be similar across conditions.

Figures 11-1 to 11-3 below show the first and second formants (F1 and F2) for individual instances of the DRESS vowel (left) and the TRAP vowel (right). A point which is higher on the plot represents a vowel where the tongue position is close to the roof of the mouth. Points towards the left represent tongue positions which are closer to the front of the mouth. Conversely, a point lower down and further to the right represents a tongue position which is lower and further back in the mouth. The spoken vowels are shown with open squares and the sung vowels are in black circles.

Figure 11-1 shows the results for Dylan, which evidence a clear separation between singing and speaking for the two vowels. For both DRESS and TRAP, the sung vowels have a lower tongue position than the spoken vowels. The pattern is the same for Andrew (as shown in fig. 11-2), the sung and spoken vowels having entirely distinct distributions of points. This confirms that for these singers, at least for the DRESS and TRAP vowels, their singing is very different to their speaking, with their sung vowels approximating an American style.

---

[11] For the sake of clarity, when discussing individual vowels, sociolinguists use labels (written with small caps) which contain the vowel in question. These vowel labels were first outlined in John C. Wells, *Accents of English* (Cambridge: Cambridge University Press, 1982).
[12] Jennifer Hay, Margaret Maclagan, and Elizabeth Gordon, *New Zealand English* (Edinburgh: Edinburgh University Press, 2008), 24.

Figure 11-3 shows the vowel positions for John, who said he has made a conscious decision to sing more in his speaking voice. The points for singing and speaking are much closer together than they are for the other two singers. For DRESS, the sung tokens have a relatively high tongue position, but the vowel is still quite distinct from the spoken examples, which have a fronted tongue position. For TRAP, the two groups of points are very close together, with some overlapping between the distributions. However, the sung and spoken vowels still follow the same pattern as for the other singers, albeit to a lesser extent. For these vowels, John has been partially successful in his attempt to use his spoken accent in singing, with the two conditions being much closer for him than for the other two singers. However, the two conditions are still fairly distinct, suggesting that, despite a conscious decision, it may be difficult to completely undo years of habit and exposure to consistently different pronunciation of the vowels in sung and spoken contexts.

# Conclusion

This paper has presented some initial results of an acoustic comparison of sung and spoken vowels. These results build on previous work describing the use of American pronunciation features by New Zealand singers. The use of acoustic measurement techniques provides detailed information about the vowels used, giving insights about the gradient nature of pronunciation. In particular, it has shown that the efforts of one singer, who stated a desire to sing in a New Zealand accent, are partially successful. His sung vowels are different from his spoken vowels, but this difference is much smaller than it is for the other two artists studied.

This paper has also suggested that the pronunciation differences between singing and speaking may be largely driven by stored memories which tightly link the established pronunciation features of popular singing with their context. The conditioning caused by prior exposure may however be disrupted by an overt act of identity, if a singer actively wishes to be associated with a certain group. In such situations there is a tension between convention and innovation, as may be the case for John in the present study.

Given the small set of data presented here, these conclusions are largely speculative. In order to further explore these issues, data for a range of linguistic variables should be collected for a large number of artists and then considered alongside an investigation of the identity constructed by each artist in their music.

# References

Carlsson, Carl Johan. "The Way They Sing It: Englishness and Pronunciation in English Pop and Rock." *Moderna Sprak* 95, no. 2 (2001): 161–68.

Coddington, Anna. "Singing as We Speak? An Exploratory Investigation of Singing Pronunciation in New Zealand Popular Music." M.A. diss., University of Auckland, 2004.

Gibson, Andy. "Non-Prevocalic /r/ in New Zealand Hip-Hop." *New Zealand English Journal* 19 (2005): 5–12.

Hay, Jennifer, Margaret Maclagan, and Elizabeth Gordon. *New Zealand English*. Edinburgh: Edinburgh University Press, 2008.

O'Hanlon, Renae. "Australian Hip Hop: A Sociolinguistic Investigation." *Australian Journal of Linguistics* 26, no. 2 (2006): 193–209.

Pierrehumbert, Janet. "The Next Toolkit." *Journal of Phonetics* 34, no. 4 (2006): 516–30.

Simpson, Paul. "Language, Culture and Identity: With (Another) Look at Accents in Pop and Rock Singing." *Multilingua* 18, no. 4 (1999): 343–67.

Trudgill, Peter. *On Dialect: Social and Geographical Perspectives*. Oxford: Blackwell, 1983.

Wells, John C. *Accents of English*. Cambridge: Cambridge University Press, 1982.

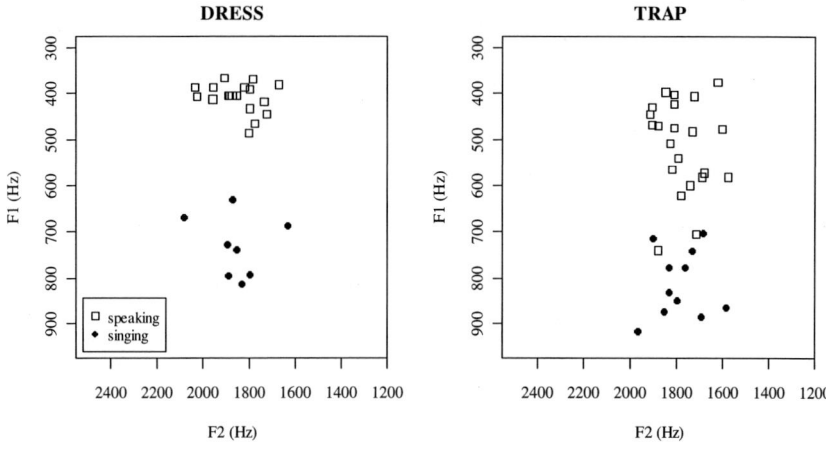

Figure 11-1. Position of sung and spoken vowels for Dylan.

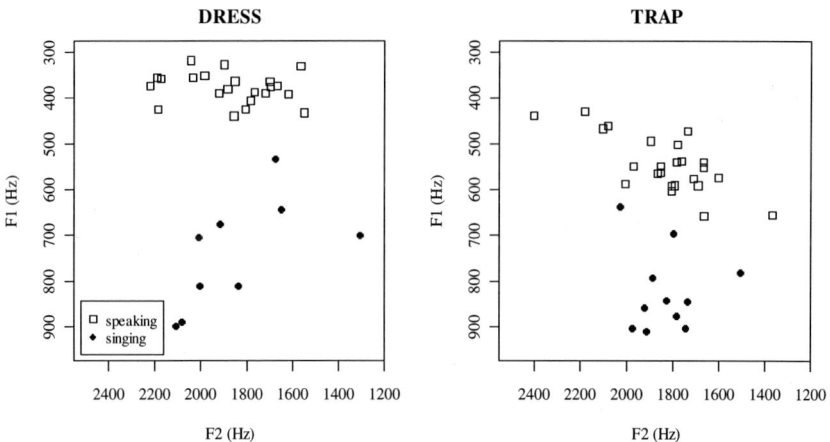

Figure 11-2. Position of sung and spoken vowels for Andrew.

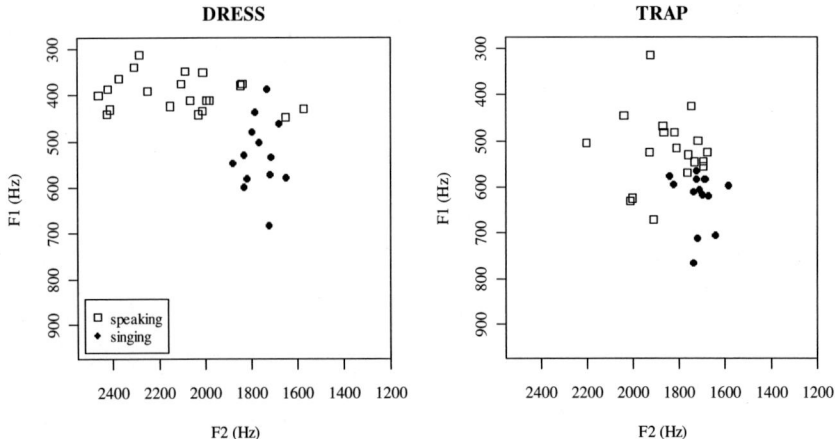

Figure 11-3. Position of sung and spoken vowels for John.

# PART III:

# EDUCATION AND HIGH ART

# CHAPTER TWELVE

# DAD LOVES HIS RUGBY, MUM'S A TAXI, AND I THINK SCHOOL IS REALLY COOL: NATIONAL IDENTITY IN THE KIWI KIDSONGS SERIES

## SALLY BODKIN-ALLEN

Children's music is not a genre that has been widely examined in New Zealand. While music education trends have been explored,[1] children's songs within the curriculum have not. This study examines a collection of children's songs created especially for New Zealand primary schools: the *Kiwi Kidsongs* (*KKs*) series. Ethnomusicologists have noted connections between children's songs and identity; in terms of both acquisition of musical style,[2] and cultural significance.[3] At the same time, popular music is part of current discourse—in regard to its relationship to identity formation, and its importance as an "indicator of cultural identity, operating at the levels of the self, community, and the nation."[4] While the songs in *KKs* are not popular music in the strictest sense of the term, they can be viewed as such because the series incorporates songs in various popular idioms (e.g., rap, rock, and country rock) as well as utilizing some songs

---

[1] See, for example, Trevor Thwaites, "Music Education in a New Key: The Dissonance of Competence, Connectedness, Culture and Curriculum," *New Zealand Journal of Research in Performing Arts and Education: Nga Mahi a Rehia* 1 (2008), http://www.drama.org.nz/ejournal; and Janet Mansfield, "The Arts in the New Zealand: From Policy to Practice" (Ph.D. diss., University of Auckland, 2000).

[2] Alan Lomax, "Musical Style and Context," *American Anthropologist* 61 (1959): 927–54.

[3] John Blacking, *Venda Children's Songs* (Chicago: University of Chicago Press, 1967) and Patricia Sheehan Campbell, *Songs in their Heads* (New York: Oxford University Press, 1998).

[4] Roy Shuker, *Understanding Popular Music Culture* (New York: Routledge, 2008), 220.

which were originally pop songs (for example, Split Enz's "Six Months in a Leaky Boat" and "Nature" by The Muttonbirds).

This paper examines the national identity that is being both created and represented in this musical resource for New Zealand school children. While *KKs* is a resource largely designed to develop classroom singing, its title, the fact that all pieces are New Zealand compositions, and its state-funded/nationwide status also suggest that it is a resource designed to convey a sense of national identity. This study is an introductory exploration of the themes relating to identity present in *KKs*.

## Background

*KKs* was first produced in 1990 and has been released every year since. It is a series of musical resources, unique to New Zealand, and distributed free to all schools throughout the country which have students at years 0–8. Learning Media, the publishing branch of the Ministry of Education, is responsible for the production and distribution of this resource. The exact format of the resource has changed over the years, reflecting changes in technology. *KKs 1* was issued as a cassette tape, for instance, with CDs not being used until *KKs 9*. Other formats have included a DVD and an enhanced CD. The songs are always prepared in two versions: one with vocals and one without.

Janice Marriott, who has been involved with the series since its inception, and has been its producer since *KKs 5*, says that it is primarily a resource designed to encourage children to sing together, and the defining characteristic of the series is the recording quality.[5] Certainly, the recordings are of a professional standard, reflecting Marriott's background in the Audio Production Unit of Learning Media. She states that the primary characteristics of the songs are that they are all written by New Zealand songwriters, are easy to sing along to, and appeal to children.

Being an educational resource, the series has also responded to the changing curriculum. The initial *KKs* came with "a leaflet of notes"[6] and this has developed over the years to become a handbook of notes for teachers, sheet music, OHP designed lyric sheets, direct links to the curriculum, and now connections to the integrated arts curriculum (dance, drama, music, and the visual arts). *KKs 16* reflects this approach to the arts and includes opportunities to expand into other areas, such as dance and

---

[5] Janice Marriott, e-mail message to author, February 25, 2008. The author would like to acknowledge and thank Janice Marriott for her contribution to this article.

[6] Marriott, e-mail message to author, February 24, 2008.

drama. This sixteenth edition in the series is also significant because it is Pacific-themed.[7] This, together with *KKs 15* (which is a collection of ten *waiata*) and the incidental songs from Māori and Pacific cultures that have been included in the series, is indicative of the bicultural and multicultural nature of *KKs*.[8] Marriott suggests that *KKs* reflects the "ethnic make up of New Zealand school children."[9]

This study is focused on the *Kiwi Kidsongs Collection* which came out in 2000 and is a twenty-two song compilation of popular songs from *KKs 1–9*. Part of the rationale for the *Collection* was that teachers were unable to order some of the older *KKs* because they were out of stock and Learning Media were often being asked for them.[10] Consequently, a questionnaire was sent out to all the schools who had contacted them over the years about *KKs* and the schools were asked to vote for their twenty favourites, from a list of all the songs.[11] The result is the *Collection* which has a total of twenty-two songs. It has been used for this study because it represents the favourites: the most popular, well known, and therefore potentially the most sung, of the *KKs* songs.

## Music and Identity

When discussing Australian identity in music, Turner suggests that it is a "waste of time" looking for signifiers of Australianness in music texts.[12] He says works are Australian on the basis of being produced, consumed, and performed there. However, Hayes believes that there is a recognisably Australian music, because of the country's unique history, location, geography, and other factors.[13] Identity can also be constructed in terms of images: of Australia's history (indigenous beginnings, convict past, recent

---

[7] *Kiwi Kidsongs 16: Pasifika Music,* Learning Media, 2009.

[8] *Kiwi Kidsongs Waiata 15: He Waiata mō ngā Kaupapa Ake*, Learning Media, 2006.

[9] Marriott, e-mail message to author, February 25, 2008.

[10] Marriott, e-mail message to author, February 24, 2008.

[11] "Teacher's Handbook," *Kiwi Kidsongs Collection* (Wellington: Learning Media, 2000), 3.

[12] Graeme Turner, "Australian Popular Music and its Contexts," in *From Pop to Punk to Postmodernism: Popular Music and Australian Culture from the 1960s to 1990s,* ed. Phillip Hayward (Sydney: Allen & Unwin, 1992), 17.

[13] Quoted in Scott Harrison, "Who'll Come a Waltzing Matilda? The Search for Identity in Australian Music Education," in *Cultural Diversity in Music Education: Directions and Challenges for the 21st Century*, ed. Patricia Shehan Campbell et al. (Brisbane: Australian Academic Press, 2005), 117.

moves towards diversity), and of its geographic features (the land, the weather, the outback).[14] This can be translated to the concept of national identity in New Zealand also; to a certain extent, our identity is associated through images of our historical and geographic features. These have developed to become national icons such as the Buzzy Bee, the gumboot, pavlovas, and summers at the beach.

Harrison examines some iconic Australian songs from the popular music canon; for example, "Sounds of Then (This is Australia)," refers to humidity, lightning flashes, and the cane fields,[15] referencing recognizable Australian occurrences. Likewise, "Down Under," with the lyrics "I come from a land down under/Where beer does flow and men chunder." While not implying that all men in Australia drink excessively and vomit, Harrison proposes a strong association of this song with the America's Cup win in 1983, together with its lyrical content, connecting "the fascination with sport, the concept of the underdog, toughness and humour."[16]

Dave Dobbyn's song "Loyal" can be viewed in a similar way in New Zealand culture. It has been associated with an America's Cup campaign (in 2003) as well as with rugby in New Zealand. For example, Dave Dobbyn sang it on a Sports Café programme to farewell All Blacks' captain Sean Fitzpatrick.[17] Harrison is searching for an identity in Australian music education and raises more questions than he answers. His main argument seems to be that only by recognizing cultural diversity in Australian music education, will music education in Australia become truly Australian.

In a New Zealand context, Shuker looks at national identity from a number of levels or layers: through the use of music consumption to indicate cultural capital, especially in subcultures (such as schools); community identity, through notions of local sounds and scenes; and national identity, through cultural policies aimed at promoting locally produced music.[18] *KKs* in some ways exemplifies this latter layer: it is certainly aimed at promoting locally-produced music. A further element in Shuker's framework is the association of particular genres and settings; he refers to the "Dunedin sound," and in *KKs* there are elements of this to

---

[14] Harrison, "Who'll Come a Waltzing Matilda?" 117.

[15] Ibid., 117.

[16] Ibid., 117.

[17] Comment on "Recent Sightings," *The D-Files*, comment posted May, 1998, http://www.geocities.com/belltower.geo/where.htm.

[18] Shuker, *Understanding Popular Music Culture*, 220.

consider. Shuker also notes that songwriters use themes of homeland and the nation to both situate and authenticate their music.

## The Songs

Of the twenty-two songs on the *Kiwi Kidsongs Collection*, six have no discernable New Zealand aspects: "School is Number One," "Hey Crocodile!," "Pirate Band," "Edith the Elf," "Silly Hat Store," and "The Brontosaurus Boogie." There are no references to anything local in these songs; rather, they are based on children's themes, and can be regarded as purely children's songs.

The next group of songs to consider have surface references in the lyrics to aspects of New Zealand identity/culture. "Fish and Chips," for example, has the lyric "I like peanut butter on my bread/Maybe marmite and honey instead," reflecting aspects of New Zealand's culinary culture. The song "My Mum's a Taxi" is a song many New Zealand parents would be able to relate to. It details the life of a busy New Zealand mum, driving her children to various daytime and after school activities, expressed in lyrics such as "and John to kindergarten and the baby to the crèche" and "on Tuesday there is netball and karate for Mark." "Sausages and Custard" is a rather humorous song that focuses on the culinary experience of a family dog that only gets leftovers mixed together. He longs for "Pal and Champ and Jellymeat," rather than cold pizza mixed in with last week's roast. This song has references to common "human" food in New Zealand, as well as dog food. The All Blacks, New Zealand's iconic rugby team, and John Hart (a former coach of the All Blacks) are referred to in "My Dad Loves his Rugby." This song also reflects on a familiar sight on Saturday mornings throughout New Zealand: that of parents standing on the side lines watching their kids play sport.

Language is also a significant feature on the *Kiwi Kidsongs Collection* in terms of reflecting New Zealand identity. There are three songs that are wholly in Māori ("Koromiko," "Mauria Mai Taku Wai," and "Uira"), as well as a song that is in Samoan ("Le 'Aute"). There are two songs that contain both Māori and English lyrics ("Y2K" and "Yesterday Tomorrow") and one song that has lyrics in Māori, English, and Samoan ("Copycat Rap"). The use of *te reo* and Samoan, together with English, reflects both biculturalism and an element of multiculturalism.

## From the Country to the Beach and into Space

"Going Down to the Country" is a song about growing up in rural New Zealand. The lyrics provide images of country life, reflecting on and recognizing the children who grow up on farms all over New Zealand. The style of this song is also significant: it is a country song, reflecting a part of our musical heritage/identity. Country music is a strong part of musical communities throughout New Zealand, such as Gore.[19] The rivalry that exists in New Zealand between "townies" and those who live in rural areas is apparent in lines such as "spent my money on junk food, down at the corner dairy/I'd rather have a square meal in my belly," and "I've got Band-Aids on my knees, from falling on the concrete/I'd rather play out in the hay instead." Along with Band Aids, gumboots and milking cows, television is referred to as "telly"; all examples of language which evoke a sense of national identity and, in the case of the latter, our British roots.

"Never Hitch a Ride with a Martian" also has examples of idiomatic language: the use of phrases such as "me and my cobbers," and "me and my mates." This song refers to a local place, Raetihi, a small town in the central North Island; as well as to the macrocarpa tree which, while not a New Zealand native, is nevertheless a species that is prevalent here. This song is in the style of a country/folk/ballad/yarn, such as those found in New Zealand and Australia. Somewhat ironically, the accompanying notes for this song suggest that it is in the style of Slim Dusty, who is an Australian. This, perhaps, is an indication of our rivalry and our connection to Australia: we are linked to Australia through our shared colonial past, but at the same time struggle to assert our own sense of identity.

"Christmas on the Beach" is a song about celebrating Christmas in New Zealand: "We don't want no holly or mistletoe/We don't want no Christmas tree with artificial snow/We don't want no snowman, made of cotton wool/We're not a bunch of fools," proclaim the lyrics. This song reflects a postcolonial New Zealand identity: the traditional pine tree has been replaced by a *pōhutukawa* tree. Many of the traditional Christmas songs sung in New Zealand represent the Northern Hemisphere idea of Christmas (such as "Deck the Halls" and "White Christmas"). This song celebrates a Kiwi kid's Christmas. The accompanying notes suggest that teachers utilize other "symbols of a NZ summer" in a musical way (such

---

[19] See, for example, Dan Bendrups and Henry Johnson, "Gore Gold Guitars: The Place of Country in New Zealand," *Perfect Beat* 8, no. 3 (2007): 52–67.

as cricket bats, sunglasses, tupperware, and a chilly bin),[20] also reinforcing the sense of identity in this song.

The song "Yesterday Tomorrow," as mentioned above, uses both English and *te reo*. The lyrical content is also reflective of Māori spiritual elements; it refers to the creation story and to *Papatuanuku* (Earth Mother). The second verse outlines the colonial history of New Zealand, while the final verse is based around New Zealand today: the message is about looking after our country through preservation and conservation. *Taonga puoro* are used on this track, giving it a sound quality that is distinctively New Zealand.

## Conclusion

To return to Turner: this music is New Zealand music because it is created, produced, and consumed here. *KKs* relates to the different levels of national identity that Shuker outlined. At the state/national level, *KKs* is significant to national identity because it is funded by the government, through the Ministry of Education. At the subcultural level, *KKs* is significant because it forms a kind of shared and recognizable repertoire for primary school children throughout New Zealand. The songs represent a category of cultural capital at the subcultural level of the school.

In *KKs*, songs are littered with references to places and people and things that are distinctly part of New Zealand culture, as well as having a sense of locality in terms of themes that New Zealand children can relate to. Just as Harrison noted that the references to cane fields and humidity in Australian songs gave them a sense of Australianness, *KKs* songs about growing up in the country, spending Christmas at the beach, and referring to Māori creation mythology provide images and themes that give these songs a sense of national identity for New Zealand school children. There is also a strong sense of identity through the use of language: Māori and Samoan languages can be heard in many of the songs on the *Collection*, and some editions of *KKs* have focused solely on Māori and Pacific songs.

However, while there is recognition and representation of Māori, Pacific, colonial, and postcolonial roots, which reflects a certain level of cultural diversity, it should be noted that the *Collection* lacks any recognition of Asian cultures in New Zealand.

Janice Marriott has said that there is no typical song for Kiwi kids. The few examples examined here reflect this. Scott Harrison suggested that only when Australian music education acknowledged and represented its

---

[20] "Teacher's Handbook," *Kiwi Kidsongs Collection*, 5.

cultural diversity would it truly represent its national identity. I think that perhaps, with *KKs*, New Zealand is on its way to doing just that.

## References

Bendrups, Dan, and Henry Johnson. "Gore Gold Guitars: The Place of Country in New Zealand." *Perfect Beat* 8, no. 3 (2007): 52–67.

Blacking, John. *Venda Children's Songs*. Chicago: University of Chicago Press, 1967.

Campbell, Patricia Sheehan. *Songs in their Heads*. New York: Oxford University Press, 1998.

Harrison, Scott. "Who'll Come a Waltzing Matilda? The Search for Identity in Australian Music Education." In *Cultural Diversity in Music Education: Directions and Challenges for the 21st Century*, edited by Patricia Shehan Campbell et al., 113–24. Brisbane: Australian Academic Press, 2005.

*Kiwi Kidsongs Collection*. Learning Media, 2000.

*Kiwi Kidsongs Waiata 15: He Waiata mō ngā Kaupapa Ake*. Learning Media, 2006.

*Kiwi Kidsongs 16: Pasifika Music*. Learning Media, 2009.

Lomax, Alan. "Musical Style and Context." *American Anthropologist* 61 (1959): 927–54.

Mansfield, Janet. "The Arts in the New Zealand: From Policy to Practice." Ph.D. diss., University of Auckland, 2000.

"Recent Sightings," *The D-Files,* http://www.geocities.com/belltower.geo/where.htm.

Shuker, Roy. *Understanding Popular Music Culture.* New York: Routledge, 2008.

Thwaites, Trevor. "Music Education in a New Key: The Dissonance of Competence, Connectedness, Culture and Curriculum." *New Zealand Journal of Research in Performing Arts and Education: Nga Mahi a Rehia* 1 (2008), http://www.drama.org.nz/ejournal.

Turner, Graeme. "Australian Popular Music and its Contexts." In *From Pop to Punk to Postmodernism: Popular Music and Australian Culture from the 1960s to 1990s*, edited by Philip Hayward, 11–24. Sydney: Allen & Unwin, 1992.

# CHAPTER THIRTEEN

# ON THE PREHISTORY OF MUSIC IN NEW ZEALAND

# ROBIN MACONIE

In 1764, Mozart traveled to London with his father. During his stay, the eight year-old prodigy was examined by Daines Barrington, a fellow of the Royal Society. He was asked to improvise recitatives and keyboard accompaniments after the conventions of Italian opera, in the Italian language, expressing a range of classic emotions such as rage, fear, hope, and joy.[1]

Eighteenth-century philosophers turned to musical forms and figures of speech as templates of universal emotional states and temperaments. Handel was brought from Italy to England in 1710 as a specialist in *opera seria*. Italy was the birthplace of opera and Italian its natural language. The volatile Italian temperament is conveyed in a speech rooted in the Latin of ancient history.

Through music, universal laws of Newtonian physics could be brought to bear on the moral and textual ambiguities of conventional drama. In opera and the baroque dance suite, archetypal behaviours and patterns of movement in space and time are made available for review under the rubric of *Affektenlehre*, the science of Affections or inherent motivations as opposed to learned behaviour.[2]

Biculturalism, in the abstract sense of how to establish relations and negotiate with remote island communities, is the subject of Daniel Defoe's

---

[1] Daines Barrington, "Account of a Very Remarkable Young Musician. In a Letter from the Honourable Daines Barrington, F.R.S. To Mathew Maty, M.D. Sec. R.S" *Philosophical Transactions* 60 (1770): 54–64.

[2] "The theory was based upon the assumption that passions or emotions [are] definite in character, concrete in form, and separable in the mind." Gary Schmidgall, *Literature as Opera* (New York: Oxford University Press, 1977), 38–39.

*Robinson Crusoe* (1719), and *Gulliver's Travels* by Dean Swift, published in 1726. In 1729, John Gay's production of *The Beggar's Opera* attacked the pretensions of *opera seria* in order to address the harsh realities of difference in relation to social inequality at home. In a souvenir engraving, William Hogarth depicts the spirit of harmony in flight, musicians as creatures of indecent morals performing on primitive instruments, and the principal characters on a makeshift stage as having the voices—and by inference, the manners, or natural affections—of wild beasts (fig. 13-1).[3]

Daines Barrington's examination of the boy Mozart can be construed as an inquiry into the essential types and forms of human emotion in their natural state, expressed in the abstract language of music and uncontaminated by adult learning. Rousseau had proclaimed a musical origin for speech, identifying tonal gesture as the primal medium of inter-species communication, more ancient than mere words which vary from region to region and are only concerned with the performance of specific tasks.

For those in authority, the power of speech was proof of divine inspiration elevating humanity above the animal kingdom, and the ruling classes over the lower orders. As the century advanced, the conventional hierarchy came under attack from civil libertarians, a growing assertiveness reflected in matching advances in musical group organization, from the small-scale *concerto grosso* model of Vivaldi and Handel (led from a keyboard) to the powerhouse of Haydn and Mozart (organized on an industrial scale and coordinated to a printed score). The post-Mannheim symphony orchestra is a model of social harmony founded on principles of universal literacy, mutual cooperation, and specialist expertise. The social implications of coordinated action on such a scale could not help but fuel the rise of revolutionary consciousness.

In planning Cook's first voyage of exploration to the Southern Ocean, the Royal Society had reason to seek out appropriate protocols of engagement with peoples living at the edge of the known world. Joseph Banks traveled with lists of key words and concepts, carefully noting the equivalent terms in the speech of isolated island communities.[4] These

---

[3] In New Zealand the word "biculturalism" refers to a sensitivity of political difference arising from language-based inequalities embedded in the Treaty of Waitangi. Such issues originally informed Royal Society deliberations on the protocols of encounter adopted on the voyages undertaken by Cook and his scientific associates.

[4] For eighteenth-century scholars and physicians such as Daines Barrington, a basic competence in music was considered essential for interpreting natural temperament and state of mind from the gestures and modes of oral communication and alien speech. Philologists such as Benjamin Franklin, Thomas

established a regime for the compilation and study of island grammars by missionaries, generating a fund of material to be zealously sifted by nineteenth-century scholars, such as Lancelot Threlkeld in New South Wales and Edward Tregear in New Zealand, in search of the fundamental particles of speech, reduced to syllables such as *pa, ta, nga, hi, ko,* etc.[5]

Comparative philology attracted educational reformers Benjamin Franklin and Samuel Johnson, also religious scholars eager to discover the ultimate meaning of biblical prophecy, and legal minds concerned for the human rights implications of language identity. Among them were Scottish jurist Lord Monboddo and naturalist and poet Erasmus Darwin— grandfather of Charles and a scion of the same family tree as Vaughan Williams. Monboddo theorized that the great apes, even though mute, deserved to be treated with the dignity due to a branch of the human family. When the Dutch anatomist Petrus Camper demonstrated that the great apes were physically unfitted for speech, the philosopher Johann Gottfried Herder saw this as divine proof that those incapable of speech were *ipso facto* unworthy of speech, and should thus be denied human status. The view of speech as an indicator of divinely-appointed rank and status, such that without language there can be no thought process or communication, was asserted by Locke, Schelling, Schopenhauer, the Oxford orientalist Archibald Sayce, the German Max Müller, and Benedetto Croce; and to this day is still invoked to impugn the intellectual competence of the deaf community.[6]

From his studies of the vocabulary of remote oral cultures, including Tahitian, Monboddo identified emphasis by syllable repetition and subtleties of vowel inflection as features of natural language corresponding to functions of rhythm, form, and accent in music. As a jurist, he was less persuaded of the contribution of melodic cadence to spoken meaning. At the request of Royal Society president Sir John Pringle, Joshua Steele corresponded with Monboddo in a dialogue leading to the publication in 1773 of Steele's *Prosodia Rationalis*, the first treatise in English to be devoted to speech melody (fig. 13-2).[7] A disciple of Irish

---

Young, and Sir William Jones were gifted musicians in addition to their exceptional linguistic attainments.

[5] Lancelot Threlkeld, "Language of the Australian Aboriginals," *Waugh's Australian Almanac, For the Year 1858* (Sydney: James W. Waugh, 1858), 60–80.

[6] "Language, it is true, is the embodiment of thought, but it is equally true that without language there can be no thought." Archibald Sayce, *Introduction to the Science of Language* (London: Kegan Paul, Trench & Trübner, 1883), 2: 305.

[7] Joshua Steele, *Prosodia Rationalis* (1773). Facs. reprint of 2nd ed. (London: 1779) (Hildesheim: Georg Olms Verlag, 1971).

elocutionist Thomas Sheridan, Steele devised a unique notation for speech, using a musical stave divided in quarter-tones, to demonstrate that analogous conventions of English stage rhetoric were objectively real and reproducible factors in communicating intention.

A compulsion to anatomize speech into its smallest units inspired efforts to reconstitute speech by mechanical means. Children's dolls that say "ma-ma" and "pa-pa" are survivals of ingenious attempts (by Erasmus Darwin in England, Kratzenfeld in Copenhagen, and von Kempelen in Vienna) to mechanize speech in the same way as musical boxes store and reproduce music.[8] Mozart, Haydn, and Beethoven were among those who composed music for mechanical reproduction; others created musical dice games, systems for composing waltzes by chance implying the mechanization of divine inspiration itself. Such imaginative devices connect the world of late eighteenth-century technical innovation directly with twentieth-century avant garde concepts of serialism, aleatoric music, artificial intelligence, computer gaming, and electronic music.

When Parliament intervened in the British East India Company and installed Warren Hastings as governor in Bengal, Samuel Johnson urged Hastings by letter to assist in the collection and preservation of Indian traditional culture.[9] Sanskrit literature had emerged as a vital link in the chain leading back to the origins of language and civilization.[10] Hastings appointed Nathaniel Brassey Halhed and, after him, William Jones, phenomenal linguists whose scholarly editions and commentaries on traditional Indian law, literature, poetry, and music would play a key role in the rise of romanticism in European culture.

After the withdrawal of Banks, Barrington nominated Johann Reinhold Forster and his son Georg Forster to join Cook on his second voyage. The German Johann Reinhold attracted criticism for intellectual coldness, and his deadpan demeanour endures as the character Spock in the television

---

[8] Bernd Pompino-Marschall, "Wolfgang von Kempelen et al.—Remarks on the History of Articulatory-Acoustic Modelling," *ZAS Papers in Linguistics* 40 (2005): 145–59.

[9] S. Johnson to Warren Hastings, Letter, March 30, 1774, in James Boswell, *Life of Samuel Johnson LL.D.* (London: J. Richardson and Co., 1823), 4: 35–36.

[10] "Care has been taken to represent their [Māori] language in a manner as simple and unembarrassed as the nature of the subject and materials would admit . . . [To] this end, the division into vowels, diphthongs and consonants as laid down in the Sanscrit Grammars, has been preferred." Samuel Lee, "Preface," in Thomas Kendall and Samuel Lee, *A New Zealand Grammar* (London: Church Missionary Society, 1820), n.p.

series *Star Trek*, a popular fiction based on Cook's voyages.[11] A native flute submitted to the Royal Society after the second voyage by Cook's associate Furneaux was examined by Joshua Steele for evidence of temperament and speech intonation, related to the scale of pitches represented by the finger holes, an approach to cultural analysis adopted by English science and eventually taken to absurd lengths by Alexander Ellis in his annotations of Helmholtz.[12] The younger Forster would go on to publish a readable and highly popular account of his travels around the world with Captain Cook, and German translations of English editions of oriental literature including the *Sakuntala* from the edition by Sir William Jones.[13] He became a celebrity and an influential advocate of social reform.

Forster's reputation as a new age advocate, who had actually encountered Māori and witnessed the *haka* being performed on the deck of the Resolution, endeared him to an intellectual elite including Goethe, Herder, and readers of his books and translations. During the 1780s, he was attached to the Vienna circle of Countess Wilhelmine, wife of Franz Joseph Thun (the son of Mozart's patron in Linz), and a patroness of Beethoven. Around 1785, Forster was inducted into the same Masonic Lodge ("Zur Wohltätigkeit") as the composer.[14] At this time, Mozart's

---

[11] An urban myth expressed in parallelisms of proper name (Captain James Cook/Captain James T. Kirk; barque *Endeavour*/Starship *Enterprise*) and mission: "to boldly go where no man has gone before."

[12] Joshua Steele, "Of a Musical Instrument, Brought by Captain Fourneaux From the Isle of Amsterdam in the South Seas, to London, in 1774, and Given to the R[oyal] S[ociety] by Joshua Steele, Esq.," *Philosophical Transactions* 5 (1775): 67. See also Hermann Helmholtz, *On the Sensations of Tone as a Physiological Basis for the Theory of Music.* 2nd rev. English ed., tr. annot. Alexander J. Ellis (1885). Reprint (New York: Dover, 1954).

[13] Georg Forster, *A Voyage Round the World in His Britannic Majesty's Sloop, Resolution, Commanded by Capt. James Cook, During the Years 1772, 3, 4, and 5,* trans. (London: White, Robson, Elmsly & Robinson, 1777). According to Andersen, a German language translation was published in 1778 (no publisher stated). I have since found a reference to a German edition published in 1787-1788 (Berlin: Haude und Spener) which may or may not be the same German edition mentioned by Andersen. The English and German versions are different editions. Sir William Jones's rendering of the *Sakuntala* by Kalidasa was published in Calcutta in 1789, and in London in 1790, but I cannot find any publisher listed. Forster's German edition (*Sakontala*) was published in Frankfurt am Main in 1791, and was much admired by Goethe and Herder.

[14] Hermann Abert, *W. A. Mozart,* tr. Stewart Spencer, ed. Cliff Eisen (Yale: Yale University Press, 2007), 783–85. Whether Mozart and Forster corresponded

German-language *singspiel*, *Die Enftuhrung aus dem Serail* (*The Abduction from the Seraglio*) signalled a radical and politically-challenging departure from operatic convention by altering Schikaneder's stereotype of the evil blackamoor to instead portray the Turkish Pascha as a figure of exemplary nobility, against the prevailing ideology of white-skinned racial superiority.[15]

In Mozart's opera *The Magic Flute* (1791), Papageno and Papagena are seen as figures of myth, their feathered costumes alluding to caged *papagaien* or lovebirds (fig. 13-3). But these creatures of nature may also be interpreted as ancestral human beings based on the images of Sydney Parkinson and William Hodges: figures with feathers in their hair, dressed in feathered cloaks, their names betraying their real status as the father and mother of humanity: *Papa* (parent), *–geno* and *–gena* (origin, race, or species).[16]

Forster's fame spread throughout Europe, as far east as the Ukraine. His translations are mentioned in Beethoven's notebooks. The slow movement theme of the *Seventh Symphony* is cited by Johannes Andersen as a lament modelled on Māori chant.[17] Listening to the repetitive stamping rhythms of the "Coriolan" overture, it is not hard to visualize a red-faced Forster demonstrating the *haka* in front of a slightly apprehensive salon gathering in Paris or Prague.[18] The same message of

---

directly remains a matter of conjecture, but the circumstantial evidence is highly indicative.

[15] Mozart was not the first composer to portray an alien ruler in a favourable light. In his opera *Montezuma* (music by Karl Heinrich Graun), premiered 1755, Frederick the Great "made of Montezuma a noble resister who would rather die than accept beliefs that were unnatural to him . . . [declaring] 'Cortez will be the tyrant.'" Christopher Hogwood, *Music at Court* (London: The Folio Society, 1977), 87–88.

[16] Clues of Papageno's Māori origin include his feathered dress, his profession of birdcatcher, his emblematic flute, and his character's wily nature (conforming to the native stereotype described by Cook, Banks, and others). Even the aria "Der Vogelfänger bin ich ja" is largely constructed within a four-note scale (F sharp, G, A, and B), a trait identified by Georg Forster as typical of native song.

[17] Johannes C. Andersen, *Maori Music*. Memoirs of the Polynesian Society, Vol. 10 (1934). Facs. repr. (Christchurch: Cadsonbury Publication, 2002), 435.

[18] Forster's description in German of the *haka* performance he witnessed on the deck of the *Resolution* is vividly rhythmical, as if intentionally to convey to German readers the energy and rhythm of the experience in real life: "Zum *Ab*schied *g*aben *un*sere *Gäs*te *uns* einen *Hiva-* oder *Kriegs*tanz zum *bes*ten, der aus *Stamp*fen mit den *Füs*sen, *droh*enden *Schwen*ken der *Keu*len und *Spee*re, *schreck*lichen Ver*zer*rungen des Ge*sicht*s, Aus*streck*ungen der *Zun*ge und *wild*em

defiance connects the short-long *iambos* of the *haka*—the primordial unequal rhythm of Greek tradition—with the "Tribal Dance of Men and Boys" from Borodin's *Polovtsian Dances*, and even the "Sacrificial Dance" of Stravinsky's *Rite of Spring*.[19]

Public opinion in England in the 1790s feared the consequences of a French-style revolution. In a poem penned in the early 1800s, Henry Kirke White, a young divinity student at Cambridge University, imagined a future lone New Zealander, a Māori counterpart of Cook or Banks, standing on Westminster Bridge and contemplating the ruins of a once great civilization.[20] Halhed and Jones had advocated tolerance, study, and respect for alien cultures.[21] Their attitude offended an emergent evangelical movement led by William Wilberforce and orchestrated from Cambridge University by Isaac Milner, Jacksonian Professor of Natural Philosophy and successor of Isaac Newton as Lucasian Professor of Mathematics. Milner's associates included elder brother Joseph Milner, John Newton (the composer of "Amazing Grace"), and firebrands Charles Simeon and Claudius Buchanan.

Isaac Milner was a chemist and mathematician whose conversion to evangelism was fuelled by a Rousseau-ian conviction that rhetoric, the musical component of speech, was a force of nature analogous to Newtonian gravitation, in the sense of a controlling "action at a distance."[22] Charles Simeon is memorialized as the Professor of Worldly Wisdom of the School of Unreason in Samuel Butler's *Erewhon*. Ecclesiastical propagandist Buchanan inveighed against "the horrid rites" of Brahma and Māori as defilements of human nature to be wiped out and

---

*Heu*len be*stand*." Italics added. Georg Forster, "Sea Voyage from the Friendly Isles to New Zealand," *Bemerkungen auf eine Reise um die Welt mit Kapitän Cook,* Kapitel 12: Entdeckungsreise nach Tahiti und in die Südsee 1772–1775, http://gutenberg.spiegel.de?id=5&xid=701&kapitel=1#gb_found.

[19] For discussion of the *iambos* see Curt Sachs, *Rhythm and Tempo: A Study in Music History* (London: J.M. Dent, 1953), 118.

[20] Henry Kirke White, author of "Time: A Poem" (c. 1803), was admired by Southey and Keats.

[21] Nathaniel Brassey Halhed's translation (from a Persian edition) of the Hindu legal code was published in London in 1776 as *A Code of Gentoo Laws*. In his "Translator's Preface," Halhed explicitly defends, for the sake of good relations and out of admiration for Indian culture, the policy of "a well-timed Toleration in Matters of Religion, and an Adoption of such original Institutes of the country, as do not immediately clash with the Laws or Interests of the Conquerors." Nathaniel Brassey Halhed, "Translator's Preface," *A Code of Gentoo Laws, or Ordinations of the Pundits* (London: n.p., 1776), ix.

[22] Isaac Milner, *An Essay on Human Liberty* (London: Ward Lock, 1820), 4–7.

purified by the moral force of the Christian faith.[23]

Together Wilberforce and Milner endorsed the appointments of Samuel Marsden and Thomas Kendall to the New Zealand mission: Marsden the rural farmer and disciplinarian, and Kendall the closet ethnologist in the tradition of Halhed and Jones. From the outset, Marsden and Kendall professed very different duties of care to the language and culture of Māori, in particular to Māori rights of self-determination in the absence of British protection at a time of significant global unrest.

Kendall's achievements in codifying Māori speech, and his historic significance as a pioneer ethnologist, have been consistently misrepresented and disparaged by New Zealand historians. He is excoriated by biographer Judith Binney and others as a loser, failure, arms dealer, and womaniser, in terms of evangelical outrage that have no place in responsible scholarship.[24] Kendall's first attempts at transcribing Māori speech were based on the Italian orthography, using accents and diacriticals to convey nuances of intonation, in conformity with Royal Society protocols and effectively reviving a medieval system of musical notation. His *A New Zealand Grammar* of 1820 incorporates a collection of eight sample Māori song texts illustrating typical emotional states: "Wai A'ta"; "Maidi Ki Te I'ngoa O Te Tama I'ti Maodi" (the service of baptism); "Pi'he" (funeral ode); "Tui" (song of the tui); "Makaukau" (kite flying song); "On Fear"; "Of a Young Woman on Being Repudiated by Her Husband"; and "Made on the Occasion of Mr Kendall's Visit to the River E Óki Anga."[25] The methodology underlying Kendall's original scheme of accentuation, of which only a tiny fragment survives, indicates respect for Māori insistence on exact intonation, awareness of the implications of Franklin's revised orthography and Monboddo's strictures on vowel nuance, and attention to

---

[23] "The passion for the Hindoo . . . seems to have been first excited by a code of Gentoo laws, transmitted with official recommendation from this country, and published at home by authority, and yet not by the code itself, but by the translator's preface, in which there are many solemn assertions impugning the Christian revelation, and giving the palm to Hindoo antiquity . . . No inhuman practices in New Zealand, or in any other newly discovered land of savages, are more offensive to natural feeling than some of those which are committed by the Hindoo people." Claudius Buchanan, *Memoir of the Expediency of an Ecclesiastical Establishment for British India* (Cambridge: Hilliard and Metcalf, 1811), 2: 23–36.

[24] Judith Binney, *Legacy of Guilt: A Life of Thomas Kendall* (Auckland: Oxford University Press, 1968).

[25] Thomas Kendall and Samuel Lee, *A Grammar and Vocabulary of the Language of New Zealand* (London: Church Missionary Society, 1820), 107–13.

the formal values attached to inflection by Joshua Steele in *Prosodia Rationalis*. A notation based on diacriticals also made sense given the limited print resources available in colonial New South Wales.[26]

Kendall's respect for Māori culture offended Marsden's evangelical principles and was met with incomprehension, withholding of funds, and abuse. Responding to complaints by Marsden to the Church Missionary Society, in 1820 Kendall found the resources to return to Cambridge University, accompanied by chiefs Hongi Hika and Hohaia Waikato, to defend his reputation in person. The party was well received and presented to the King. Their adviser Professor Samuel Lee, a former protege of Claudius Buchanan, fully appreciated Kendall's motives and scholarly intentions. As a public gesture of moral support, Lee secured Kendall's immediate elevation to the ministry during his stay, and saw to it that the new edition of *A New Zealand Grammar* was published without delay. Lee's carefully worded editorial preface reads as a barely disguised admonition directed against Kendall's detractors in the Church Missionary Society.[27]

During their brief stay, the party encountered Baron Philippe de Thierry, a refugee from the revolution in France and a mature student at Cambridge. De Thierry nurtured dreams of ruling his own South Sea principality, volunteering a substantial deposit of funds that provoked the wily Hongi to purchase arms and wage a Napoleonic war of conquest among his own people on his return. De Thierry was also musically trained. The crucial question is whether he contrived to gain access to the

---

[26]   E. Pùrenghi ki té [c] Atuà
Mo té [q] Ata
E. Jehovah ra té [c]Atuà Niui Na [q]au i
mái ngha meà katoa kidúngha ki te
Ranghi me ngha taongha katoa o raro
o te Uenua.
The above fragment reproduced by Binney, "A Prayer to God for Morning," from an unpublished manuscript "The New Zealanders First Prayers" (1819), is clear evidence of a system of diacriticals to aid pronunciation and inflection. A distinction of Kendall's system is the addition of letters *c* and *q* (newly superfluous in Franklin's revised alphabet) to the range of diacriticals used to indicate problematic aspirates (a practice that survives in use of the letter "q" for the sound "ng" in Fijian, as in the name Qarase). Binney, *Legacy of Guilt*, 180. See also C. Abdy Williams, *The Story of Notation* (London: Walter Scott, 1903), 19–23.

[27]   "When the unfavourable circumstances are considered, under which the materials have been collected and the Work composed, it is hoped that it will be found not to fall very far short of reasonable expectation." Samuel Lee, "Preface," in Kendall and Lee, *A New Zealand Grammar*, ix.

party on a pretext of transcribing Māori song into musical notation.
A reason for asking is the mysterious insertion of a paper on Māori music by James Arthur Davies, an alumnus of Trinity College Cambridge, as an appendix to Sir George Grey's *Polynesian Mythology*, published in 1855 (fig. 13-4).[28] The substance of Davies' contribution is a selection of Māori songs, allegedly dictated by Māori of high rank. The songs represent distinct emotional types in a range consistent with, though not identical to, the song texts appended to Kendall's *A New Zealand Grammar* of 1820. All are expensively engraved, but in an obsolete music typeface identical with one introduced by Breitkopf in the 1750s and anachronistic a century later. More to the point, the conventions of typesetting have been modified to indicate quarter-tones. These are not only the earliest printed specimens of Māori song in music notation, they are also the first notations of any music in quarter-tones. In his book, Grey has nothing to add about Davies or the provenance of the Māori songs, which remains a mystery. We do not know of any visit to Cambridge by high-ranking Māori between 1820 and 1854. The songs are unattributed.

Davies was admitted to Trinity College in 1826, which makes him a contemporary of Robert Willis—the latter destined to succeed Isaac Milner as Jacksonian Professor of Natural Philosophy, on the basis of influential research papers "On Vowel Sounds," published in 1828, and "On the Mechanism of the Larynx," published in 1829. If it were to transpire that the Māori songs published by Davies in his own name were recovered from Cambridge University archives relating to the 1820 visit, and had originally been intended for publication in *A New Zealand Grammar*, it would not be surprising for the Church Missionary Society to have rejected such important material, since to include it would be to admit that the Society had been wrong about Kendall, and to set a dangerous precedent of respect for Māori culture.

---

[28] Of native song encountered at Tahiti in 1773, Forster wrote: "The whole music, both vocal and instrumental, consisted of three or four notes, which were between half and quarter tones, being neither whole tones nor semitones." Georg Forster, *Voyage Round the World*, 2: 291–92. See also James A. Davies, *On the Native Songs of New Zealand* (London: Woodfall & Kinder, 1854). Repr. as App. I in Sir George Grey, *Polynesian Mythology and Ancient Traditional History of the New Zealanders* (London: Trübner, 1855).

# References

Abert, Hermann. *W.A. Mozart*. Translated by Stewart Spencer, edited by Cliff Eisen. Yale: Yale University Press, 2007.

Andersen, Johannes C. *Maori Music*. Memoirs of the Polynesian Society, Vol. 10 (1934). Facs. repr. Christchurch: Cadsonbury Publication, 2002.

Barrington, Daines. "Account of a Very Remarkable Young Musician. In a Letter from the Honourable Daines Barrington, F.R.S. To Mathew Maty, M.D. Sec. R. S." *Philosophical Transactions* 60 (1770): 54–64.

Binney, Judith. *The Legacy of Guilt: A Life of Thomas Kendall*. Auckland: Oxford University Press, 1968.

Boswell, James. *The Life of Samuel Johnson LL.D.* 4 vols. London: J. Richardson and Co., 1823.

Buchanan, Claudius. *Memoir of the Expediency of an Ecclesiastical Establishment for British India*. 2 vols. Cambridge: Hilliard and Metcalf, 1811.

Davies, James A. *On the Native Songs of New Zealand*. London: Woodfall & Kinder, 1854). Repr. as App. I in Sir George Grey, *Polynesian Mythology and Ancient Traditional History of the New Zealanders*. London: Trübner, 1855.

Forster, Georg. *A Voyage Round the World in His Britannic Majesty's Sloop, Resolution,Commanded by Capt. James Cook, During the Years 1772, 3, 4, and 5*. English ed. 2 vols. London: B. White, J. Robson, P. Elmsly & G. Robinson, 1777. German ed. 2 vols. 1778-1788.

—. "Sea Voyage from the Friendly Isles to New Zealand." *Bemerkungen auf eine Reise um die Welt mit Kapitän Cook*. Kapitel 12: Entdeckungsreise nach Tahiti und in die Südsee 1772–1775, http://gutenberg.spiegel.de?id=5&xid=701&kapitel=1#gb_found.

Grey, Sir George. *Polynesian Mythology and Ancient Traditional History of the New Zealanders*. London: Trübner, 1855.

Halhed, Nathaniel Brassey. *A Code of Gentoo Laws*. London: n.p., 1776.

Helmholtz, Hermann. *On the Sensations of Tone as a Physiological Basis for the Theory of Music*. 2nd rev. English ed., translated and annotated by Alexander J. Ellis (1885). Reprint. New York: Dover, 1954.

Hogwood, Christopher. *Music at Court*. London: The Folio Society, 1977.

Jones, William. *Sakuntala*. English ed. Calcutta: 1789; London: 1790. German ed., translated and annotated by Forster. Frankfurt am Main: 1791.

Kendall, Thomas, and Samuel Lee. *A New Zealand Grammar*. London: Church Missionary Society, 1820.

Milner, Isaac. *An Essay on Human Liberty.* London: Ward Lock, 1820.

Pompino-Marschall, Bernd. "Wolfgang von Kempelen et al.—Remarks on the History of Articulatory-Acoustic Modelling." *ZAS Papers in Linguistics* 40 (2005): 145–59.

Sachs, Curt. *Rhythm and Tempo: A Study in Music History.* London: J.M. Dent, 1953.

Sayce, Archibald. *Introduction to the Science of Language.* 2 vols. London: Kegan Paul, Trench & Trübner, 1883.

Schmidgall, Gary. *Literature as Opera.* New York: Oxford University Press, 1977.

Steele, Joshua. "Of a Musical Instrument, Brought by Captain Fourneaux From the Isle of Amsterdam in the South Seas, to London, in 1774, and Given to the R[oyal] S[ociety] by Joshua Steele, Esq." *Philosophical Transactions* 5 (1775): 67–71.

—. *Prosodia Rationalis* (1773). Facs. reprint of 2nd ed. (London: 1779). Hildesheim: Georg Olms Verlag, 1971.

Threlkeld, Lancelot. "Language of the Australian Aboriginals." In *Waugh's Australian Almanac, For the Year 1858*, 60–80. Sydney: James W. Waugh, 1858.

Williams, C. Abdy. *The Story of Notation.* London: Walter Scott, 1903.

Figure 13-1. William Hogarth: *The Beggars' Opera* (1729).

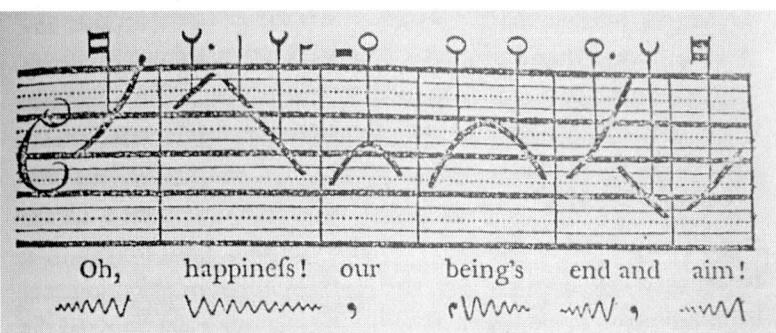

Figure 13-2. Fragment of speech notation from *Prosodia Rationalis* by Joshua Steele.

Figure 13-3. Mozart's librettist Emanuel Schikaneder costumed as Papageno for the first performance of *The Magic Flute*.

Figure 13-4. "Terate pukohu mau tonu mai:" fragment from the paper by James A. Davies as inserted in Sir George Grey's *Polynesian Mythology* (1854).

CHAPTER FOURTEEN

"GUANTI: MAN & MUSICOLOGIST" BY DENIS
GLOVER AND G.E. [GEOFFREY] FAIRBURN:
SPEAKING UP FOR NEW ZEALAND MUSIC—
A DECONSTRUCTION

MARIAN POOLE

Maestro Guanti recently passed through Wellington practically (and
characteristically) unknown except to those who have scaled the keyboard
of Academe . . . en route to Scott base on yet another musicological
expedition, festooned with tapes.
But, in more knowledgeable corners of the Free World of Music, Deniso
Guanti's is a name to conjure with.[1]

In 1969, discovering the true way forward for Western Art Music was
the *cause célèbre*. Academe had, by and large, adopted the voice from the
1920s of Schoenberg and the Second Viennese School and subsequent
advances made by such composers as Stockhausen and Boulez. The avant
garde dismissed Romantic tonality as old hat and instead ventured into a
new and, as Guanti's travel plans suggest, inhospitable world of atonality.
By 1969, this search was supported by electronic technology and tape
recorders. Academe also supported the harmonic world of composers,
such as Vaughan Williams and Aaron Copland, who accepted the need for
change but, acknowledging the role of the past (expressed, for example,
through folk music) in determining the future, advanced freely along
traditional lines. A schism had developed between the two groups,
epitomized by the difference between the seriously funny Hoffnung and

---

[1] Denis Glover and Geoffrey E. Fairburn, "Guanti—Man and Musicologist," *New
Zealand Listener*, June 20, 1969, 8.

the serious Darmstadt Festivals.[2] Broadly speaking, while the avant garde
appealed to the educated music connoisseur, an elite coterie; those
working in a tonal language appealed to the amateur music-lover, the
average concert-goer.

In 1969, the art music scene in New Zealand, encapsulated by events in
Wellington, was at a crossroads. Unsure of their own voice, local
musicologists and musicians were searching, on the one hand, for a unique
New Zealand voice independent of passing foreign influences, and, on the
other hand, for direction from the right sort of foreign expertise. Composer
Ashley Heenan, for example, while making something of a living from
local radio and theatre, looked forward to a time when "European
influences and modes of thought will be thoroughly assimilated and given
utterance in a distinct national idiom."[3]

Jenny McLeod's success with atonality at Darmstadt was equaled by
*Earth & Sky*'s successful "fus[ion] of Maori chant with medieval
organum," which was written for amateur and professional musicians and
premiered in Masterton, the home of your average New Zealander.[4] This
fluency in many languages would give McLeod local authority with both
the average concert-goer and the elite coterie.[5] However, she also
questioned the relevance of seeking foreign approval for something which
had sprung out of the New Zealand environment: "I don't feel the country
is isolated any longer, even musically; the international vocabulary is
available, through records, and radio and scores by airmail, but many

---

[2] Three Hoffnung Festivals were held at the Royal Festival Hall in London in
1956, 1958, and 1961 (after Gerald Hoffnung's death in 1959). Hoffnung's
cartoons of musicians, conductors, and choirs, exhibited first at the Festival of
Britain in 1951, continued to amuse many in England and New Zealand.

[3] Bruce Mason, "Mainly Music," *New Zealand Listener*, February 28, 1969, 15.

[4] McLeod's "For Seven" (1966) was performed by Stockhausen's ensemble at
Cologne, Darmstadt and Berlin. While in Cologne, an environment she did not
particularly enjoy, Jenny McLeod "discovered" Richard Taylor's translation of
Māori creation poetry in the *Penguin Book of New Zealand Verse*, which she had
taken with her on her travels. Allen Curnow, ed. and introd., *The Penguin Book of
New Zealand Verse* (Harmondsworth: Penguin Books, 1960); Jennifer McLeod,
"Jenny McLeod," *SOUNZ: Centre for New Zealand Music*,
http://sounz.org.nz/contributor/composer1071; Peter Platt, "Music and the Future
Role of the QEII Arts Council," *Ascent* 1, no. 3 (1969): 43. Platt's inaugural
speech as Professor of Music at Otago was published in 1959. Peter Platt, *Music
History as a Living Study: An Inaugural Lecture Delivered Before the University
of Otago on 20 September 1957* (Dunedin: University of Otago Press, 1959).

[5] McLeod succeeded Page as Professor of Music at Victoria University in 1971.
McLeod, "Jenny McLeod."

talented New Zealanders cannot be certain of their gift until it is measured and tested abroad."[6]

Alexander MacLeod, editor of the *New Zealand Listener*, wrote "Singing a Silent Song" in which he noted the increasing use of silence as a "revolt against [music] revolutionaries."[7] Cage's *Silent Sonata*[8] and Dr Schnebel's work for conductor without orchestra, *Nostalgie*,[9] were, MacLeod reported, inspired by the thought that "sound could no longer be inflicted on concert audiences."[10] As MacLeod rather peevishly said: "To those who think the only way to serve the public is to give them what they like, here is the perfect democratic solution: if they don't like silent Schoenberg they can have silent something else."[11] The all-or-nothing scenario had become threateningly real to a conservative audience.

Douglas Lilburn, New Zealand's only "serious" composer,[12] due to his ability to conjure things local with such works as *Prodigal Country, Aotearoa Overture*, and "Sings Harry" (a setting of Glover's poem), was about to take leave from his position with Frederick Page at Victoria University to study recent developments in electronic music at Toronto with Gustav Ciamaga.[13] Except for McLeod's incompletely articulated reservations, New Zealand musicians seemed primed to assimilate European tastes and, by association, foreign avant garde. An interview with Guanti was timely:

> Two foremost experts in the field, (we [Glover and Fairburn] modestly claim), who despite a technical hitch in their apparatus, assure you on their academic oath that, having been graciously accorded the unheard of

---

[6] Mason, "Mainly Music," February 28, 1969, 15.

[7] No relation to Jenny McLeod.

[8] Listed by Pritchett and Kuhn as "4′ 33″, tacit for any inst/insts, 1952." James Pritchett and Laura Kuhn, "Cage, John," in *Grove Music Online. Oxford Music Online*, 2009, http://www.oxfordmusiconline.com.

[9] Paul Attinello, "Schnebel, Dieter Wolfgang (B1930)," in *Grove Music Online. Oxford Music Online*, 2009, http://www.oxfordmusiconline.com.

[10] Alexander MacLeod, "Singing a Silent Song," *New Zealand Listener*, February 21, 1969, 5.

[11] Ibid.

[12] Owen Jensen, "'Music in a Cold Climate': Review of New Zealand Composers. A Series of Twelve Radio Talks Compiled for the YC Programme NZBC," *New Zealand Listener*, November 1, 1968, 11.

[13] Works which Lilburn attributes to his sabbatical in Toronto included "5 Toronto Pieces" (1963 and 1969), "Summer Voices" (1969), "Three Studies for Gustav Ciamaga" (1969). Philip Norman, *Douglas Lilburn: His Life and Work* (Christchurch: Canterbury University Press, 2006), 241.

privilege of an interview which they are now permitted to make public for the first time, this is, stave and clef, a fair and accurate account of it.[14]

Denis Glover, New Zealander writer and our conjurer, founded The Caxton Press which published *Islands* and *Landfall*, the first journals to deal exclusively with serious New Zealand culture. He was known for being proudly subversive and impatient with, among other things, pretense and officialdom.[15] A drinking and betting man, he embodied New Zealand's iconic national character. Geoffrey Fairburn (brother of Arthur Rex Dugard Fairburn)[16] was an artist and writer, known for his skeptical views on New Zealand culture. In the 1960s, Fairburn was reviewing cultural events for the Waikato Times:

> Maestro Guanti, we report, is an ebullient little man . . . As a foreigner, he gives off to our ears, a faint whiff of patchouli; the scraps of cannelloni adding grace notes to his tartan velveteen waistcoat merely emphasize his universality—he could, in fact be your average New Zealander, car salesman, cabinet minister, university lecturer, insurance agent.[17]

Working hand-in-glove with Glover, Guanti is a hybrid, a synchrony, or simply a cacophonous pastiche. He also acts as a catalyst and a warning. By sleight of hand and with an allusion to the tramp in "Sings Harry,"[18] Guanti embodies the socially aspirant New Zealander, who, by straining to assimilate foreign idioms, risks making a mockery of his own:

> He commands two languages fluently, with a musicianly [sic] disdain for syntax or grammar.
> Enough of the man. We came straight to the nub.
> "What, Maestro [Guanti], do you think of the modern movement?"
> He plucked a pizzicato ruminatively on an armpit for several moments. "In musics is no other," he announced.
> "But," we urged—

---

[14] Glover and Fairburn, "Guanti—Man and Musicologist," 8.

[15] Gordon Ogilvie, "Glover, Denis James Mathews 1912–1980," in *Dictionary of New Zealand Biography* (Wellington: Ministry of Culture and Heritage, 2007), http://www.dnzb.govt.nz.

[16] Geoffrey Earl Fairburn, *Growing Up With Rex: A Memoir 1903–1923* (Hamilton, New Zealand: Geoffrey E. Fairburn, 1991).

[17] Glover and Fairburn, "Guanti—Man and Musicologist," 8.

[18] Lilburn's setting of "Sings Harry" was premiered in 1953.

"No such thing." He cut in swiftly. "Boulez and Stockhausen say it, and now I repeat it—fall down the opera house, give it to Sydney, unband the orchestra, strangle all vocalists, do away the audience. Sono finito!"
"—and the decadent tradition of the west consigned to the oblivion it so deservedly brought upon itself?"
"E giusto! Is right!" he cried.
"And what," we suggested slyly, "of the universities?"
He laughed merrily. "Che differente! How you say it, a different horse colour? Naturellement, we have the professor. How else the student know what they not listen to?"[19]

In March 1969, Richard Hoffmann (Schoenberg's nephew and amanuensis then collating Schoenberg's archives) was passing through New Zealand on a family visit. He took the opportunity to reiterate material from earlier articles "A Note on Schoenberg" published in *Music Ho* (1948)[20] and "The New Music" published in the *New Zealand Listener* (1957)[21] which coincided with his lecture tour of New Zealand University campuses at the invitation of Professor Page. On this occasion, Hoffmann gave a radio broadcast, "Schoenberg: Man and Musicologist," and published an article, "Schoenberg: The Man of 'Moses.'"[22] Hoffmann asked, "What would have happened to New Zealand music if Arnold Schoenberg had come here to settle in 1945?" Having already assessed the country's beauty from his stamp collection, Schoenberg had enquired after the local cost of employing at least one servant. Schoenberg did not become a New Zealander, but settled in Los Angeles where he continued, as Hoffmann said, "uncompromisingly forging ahead, regardless of failure or success, along the road he knew it was his destiny to take."[23] Hoffmann's presentation of a quote from Schoenberg reveals that Schoenberg had assumed a role not unlike that of Moses: "It would be impossible to prevent the young and gifted from emulating his style—'for in ten years every talented composer will be writing in this way, regardless of whether he has learnt it directly from me or only from my works.'"[24]
Despite enjoying a small but devoted audience, the avant garde hankered after the conservative concert stage. Without significant success,

---

[19] Glover and Fairburn, "Guanti—Man and Musicologist," 8.
[20] Richard Hoffmann, "A Note on Schoenberg," *Music Ho* 7, no. 4 (1948): 5.
[21] Richard Hoffman, "The New Music," *New Zealand Listener*, August 23, 1957, 30.
[22] Richard Hoffman, "Schoenberg: The Man of 'Moses,'" *New Zealand Listener*, March 7, 1969, 11.
[23] Ibid.
[24] Ibid.

they had grown to despise those responsible for ensuring the survival of such monuments to tradition. Schoenberg had believed that at some metaphorical time "when parallel lines meet," he would gain recognition from these echelons.[25] The real task of educating the new middle-classes to appreciate Schoenberg's true music had fallen, appropriately enough, to the universities. Hoffmann and Page were his strongest advocates or disciples and, as Glover would have it, his servants in New Zealand.

Since the mid 1930s and before he met Hoffmann, Frederick Page distinguished himself through his penchant for things risqué. As an undergraduate at Canterbury, he had instigated the performance of Orff's *Carmina Burana*, performed and analyzed Berg's *Piano Sonata* Op. 1,[26] got offside with his lecturer Dr Bradshaw, who taught harmony according to the accepted authorities of the day such as Kitson and the Bach Chorales,[27] and got onside with Otto Frankel, a wartime refugee and Schoenberg's associate. Page also kept up with events at Darmstadt and was accustomed to producing lists of avant garde composers with which to challenge critics of Schoenberg's Modernity,[28] such as the arch-conservative Louis Daly Austin who was only too ready to rise to the bait.[29] In the late 1940s, Professor Galway (from Otago), being less vociferous than Austin, had, Page observed, been "visibly shaken," by Page's assertion that, if it were not for Schoenberg, Vaughan Williams' *Sixth Symphony* would not have been written.[30] In his professional capacity at Victoria, Page would assess New Zealand student composers

---

[25] The notion is entertained in Schoenberg's *Style and Idea* (Williams & Norgate, 1951), 164–65, and forms the unresolved dramatic tension in *Moses und Aron* (unfinished).

[26] Frederick Page, "Some Twentieth-Century Pianoforte Music: No. 2, Sonata for Piano Opus 1. Alban Berg," *Music Ho* 2, no. 4 (1942): 3.

[27] Charles H. Kitson: *The Elements of Musical Composition* (London: Oxford University Press, 1936); *Studies in Fugue* (London: Clarendon Press, 1928).

[28] The first of these appeared in print in the monthly magazine *Music in New Zealand* as a reply to conservative music writer Louis Daly Austin. Frederick Page, "Correspondence," *Music in New Zealand* 3, no. 9 (1933): 8.

[29] Louis Daly Austin: "Is Modern Music Decadent," *Music in New Zealand* 3, no. 7 (1933): 3; "This Modern Stuff and Other Things," *Music Ho* 4, no. 4 (1946): 14–15; "The Musical Climate: Letters from Listeners," *New Zealand Listener*, June 6, 1957, 11.

[30] Frederick Page, *Frederick Page: A Musician's Journal, 1905–1983*, ed. and arranged by John Mansfield Thomson and Janet Paul (Dunedin: J. McIndoe, 1986), 101. Vaughan Williams' *Sixth Symphony* was composed in 1947, first recorded in 1949, and revised in 1950.

according to their assimilation of the avant garde sound.[31] In 1969, his list of twentieth-century classics included Schoenberg, Debussy, Berg, Webern, Ives, Bartók, and Varèse. His list of "our contemporaries" included Stravinsky, Messiaen, and Lutoslawski.[32] He did not include those New Zealanders such as Tremain[33] and McLeod who were winning recognition overseas for their serial voices. It was time for Glover and Fairburn to look the gift horse in the mouth:

"Tell us about your own compositions."
"Bene! Bene! Excellent!" he became animated. "First my early works, beginning this year"—and here he excitedly whipped out a slightly soiled envelope (since bequeathed by me to the as yet unplanned school of music in the University of Patea)[34] and scribbled the opening bars below. [fig. 14-1]
"Truly a cataclysmic utterance" we enthused, "More! More!"
The great man replied simply, "Is no more! Is all."
We freely admit we were visibly shaken by such musicological integrity. Glover's hand trembled as he tucked this immortal seed of an unknown work into the flyover of his rental pinstripes.
"More, More!" we begged . . . [fig. 14-2]
It was with awe that we observed in one rapid glance the staggering architectonics adumbrating in the few simple notes he feverishly dashed on the back of a well-used vice-regal invitation which Glover found in his side pocket . . . But what of your latest work, Maestro, we urged, "What of that?"
"This only," he said quietly. "The rest, the most—e silenzio." [fig. 14-3]
"Tell us about other modern composers," we begged . . .
"Is none."
Fairburn irrupted crudely, "you are not saying then that Stravinsky, Webern, Varèse, Lutoslawski, Penderecki, Dallapiccola, Piccolomini,—all these modern titans—are *Vieux Chapeaux*?"
"As I hear it."

---

[31] Frederick Page, "Some New Zealand Composers," *Landfall* 9, no. 1 (1955): 85.

[32] Specific works included Debussy's *La Mer* and *Images*, Schoenberg's *Five Orchestral Pieces*; Ives' *Fourth of July* and *Central Park in the Dark*; Stravinsky's *Persephone*, *Symphony in C*, *Oedipus Rex*, and *Threni*; Dallapiccola's *Canti di Prigioni*; Webern's *Second Cantata*; Boulez's *Soleil des Eaux*; Nono's *Il Canto Sospeno*; and Penderecki's *St Luke Passion*. Frederick Page, "Alert at the Concert," *New Zealand Listener,* April 24, 1969, 3.

[33] John Mansfield Thomson, "Tremain, Ronald," in *Grove Music Online. Oxford Music Online*, 2009, http://www.oxfordmusiconline.com.

[34] Patea is a rural township of New Zealand not unlike Masterton. It is the second largest town in South Taranaki. Though an important settlement during New Zealand's Land Wars, in 1969 it was known primarily for its freezing works.

. . .
Fairburn recollected in time the advice of a foremost dilettante of the arts, Barouche Maison; when in doubt, talk fast and don't answer questions.
"But there must be some other moderns," Fairburn plunged on, tossing out names like milk biscuits. "What of the Russian, Beria, of Ligeti, what of Harpic from Titograd and Svengalic from Domodossola?" It was a veritable roll-call of the avant-garde. "What of Ives, Piston, Cage, Vaso da Notte, Broccolo, Grubelfinger?"
"I know them all . . . e nulla, is not nothing."[35]

Fairburn adopts Page's propensity for lists, but, as observed by Glover, takes his lead from Bruce Mason. Mason (aka Barouche Maison)[36] was the music columnist for the *New Zealand Listener* who would become best known for his *End of the Golden Weather* which toured the country and became the iconic New Zealand play. In May 1969, Mason took Hoffmann's question for, as Glover saw it, a bit of a ride on the House of Parliament.[37] Had Schoenberg taken New Zealand residency and benefitted from the healthy climate, he would, Mason proposed, have lived into his 91$^{st}$ year (1965) and bestowed the nation with cultural pride based on foreign standards and something of an official voice. Rt. Hon. Peter Frazer, New Zealand's Prime Minister, who, Mason thought, was "most hospitable to the arts," would have been overheard to say that there was "nothing like a spot of Sprechstimme after a grueling day in the House." "[Frazer] might well have decided to give Schoenberg everything he needed . . . round a man of hugely creative powers . . . a whole native school of composers, the envy of the world, might well have grouped."[38]
Mason's freewheeling and Fairburn's fast-talk dismantle Page's authority. Those from Academe might know that Piccolomini lived during the sixteenth century;[39] Lavrentii Beria is remembered as one of the cruelest leaders in the Bolshevik regime,[40] but the name bears an uncanny resemblance to Berio, one of the tight-circle of Darmstadt-ian electronic composers;[41] "Harpic" might refer to the popular movie comedian and

---

[35] Glover and Fairburn, "Guanti—Man and Musicologist," 8.
[36] Barouche Maison translates as "house carriage."
[37] Bruce Mason, "Mainly Music," *New Zealand Listener*, May 2, 1969, 15.
[38] Ibid.
[39] William F. Prizer, "Piccolomini, Niccolò," in *Grove Music Online. Oxford Music Online*, 2009, http://www.oxfordmusiconline.com/subscriber/article/grove/music/51876.
[40] "Lavrentiy Beria," *Wikipedia*, 2009, http://en.wikipedia.org/wiki/Lavrentiy_Beria.
[41] The Darmstadt tight circle included Stockhausen, Ligeti, Maderna, and Boulez.

harpist and pianist, Harpo Marx of the Marx Brothers, or to a local brand of cleaning agent, or be the name given to a Russian cocktail drink; the fictional character Svengali was an hypnotist and here a potentially bad-mouthed teacher who dominated his students; Domodossola, a town in Italy, could also refer to a doss house, a shelter to the homeless; Vaso de Notte—I'll leave to your imagination. Guanti continues:

> "Basta! Che Buffo!," he exclaimed, "But I forget! What of Professore Feodoriko Fattorino and his, how you say it cereal musics? And not to forget, Professor Dougal Dilhorn?"
> "Great fellows, great fellows," we agreed heartily, "but too busy to compose. In any case they are unfortunately both absent from the country—either taking annual sabbatical leave or lecturing on you in your own country."[42]

Lilburn, seen here by Glover as something of an absent-minded country boy, was indeed preparing to leave New Zealand, and, while not as productive as he had been in Canterbury or as he would be after his return from Toronto, he had not abandoned the notion of a uniquely New Zealand voice. In March 1969, Lilburn was giving an open lecture at the University of Otago.[43] Having a foot in both camps, Lilburn acknowledged that he had "no grand conclusions to offer" to the "complexities of the contemporary international scene."[44] On the one hand, he believed "the innumerable creative manifestations of our total way of life are . . . affirmations of our tradition."[45] On the other hand, he believed "in preferring to search the unpleasant or unpalatable truths of his own experience, I think [the NZ composer] has the best chance of discovering the sources of his creativity, whatever larger thing may give validity to his choice of language."[46]

Page, arguing from his office at Victoria in the heart of Wellington, was absent in a more figurative sense. Glover sees him, pedagogically speaking, as a little messenger boy in service to false prophets and mindless of the New Zealand product in a very real and purposeful sense.

---

[42] Glover and Fairburn, "Guanti—Man and Musicologist," 8.

[43] Douglas Lilburn, *A Search for a Language: Open Lecture 12 March 1969 at University of Otago* (Wellington: Alexander Turnbull Library Endowment Trust; New Zealand Composers Foundation, 1985).

[44] Ibid., 22.

[45] Ibid., 22.

[46] Ibid., 22.

The result being that Glover and Fairburn, our "the two foremost experts in the field," are unaware of local leading figures. As Guanti said:

"You never know, amico mio, as I do that to hear Paggio and Alexinski, play their silent sonata is to see it all?"
Shamed, a little confused, we confessed our ignorance. Who were these legendary figures? He shrugged contemptuously,
"Forse, sono pedagogi. No matter are not important" He muttered and would say no more.[47]

Alex Lindsay's early career in the New Zealand Federation of Chamber Music, the New Zealand branch of the ISCM,[48] his own String Orchestra and leadership of the National Orchestra, was rewarded in 1959 with an MBE. Ten years later, the impact he made on the New Zealand music scene was, as Glover and Fairburn would have it, subsumed by Page's dedication to Falstaffian masters.[49]

While the New Zealand voice (expressed by Heenan, McLeod, and Lilburn, and represented here by Fairburn and Glover) rubbed shoulders with that of Page, Hoffmann, and Schoenberg (represented here by Guanti), the difference between those who fawn and those who pontificate remains slight. However, the very existence of the skit and the fact that it was published after some six months of debate over the value of contemporary music suggests that the average concert-goer was, like Alexander MacLeod, prepared to stand up for what they knew and liked and no longer prepared to be patronized. While this skit might have its origins in the British comedy show *Beyond the Fringe* or in the Hoffnung Festivals,[50] it is a uniquely New Zealand revolt against the revolutionaries. The cultural standoff is defused through having its absurdity highlighted. The many voices in the skit make fun and nonsense out of an impasse in the development of a single New Zealand voice and indeed point to the implausibility of that notion.

---

[47] Glover and Fairburn, "Guanti—Man and Musicologist," 8.

[48] International Society for Contemporary Music.

[49] Paggio is Falstaff's page in Verdi's opera *Falstaff*.

[50] The comedians included Jonathan Miller, Dudley Moore, Peter Cook, and Alan Bennett. Recordings of "Beyond the Fringe" were available in New Zealand in 1969.

# References

Attinello, Paul. "Schnebel, Dieter Wolfgang (B1930)." In *Grove Music Online*. *Oxford Music Online*, 2009, http://www.oxfordmusiconline.com.

Austin, Louis Daly. "Is Modern Music Decadent?" *Music in New Zealand* 3, no. 7 (1933): 3.

—. "The Musical Climate: Letters from Listeners." *New Zealand Listener*, June 6, 1957, 11.

—. "This Modern Stuff and Other Things." *Music Ho* 4, no. 4 (1946): 13–15.

Curnow, Allen, ed. and introd. *The Penguin Book of New Zealand Verse*. Harmondsworth: Penguin Books, 1960.

Fairburn, Geoffrey Earl. *Growing Up With Rex: A Memoir 1903–1923*. Hamilton, New Zealand: Geoffrey E. Fairburn, 1991.

Glover, Denis, and Geoffrey E. Fairburn. "Guanti Man and Musicologist." *New Zealand Listener*, June 20, 1969, 8.

Hoffmann, Richard. "A Note on Schoenberg." *Music Ho* 7, no. 4 (1948): 5.

—. "Schoenberg: The Man of 'Moses.'" *New Zealand Listener*, March 7, 1969, 11.

—. "The New Music." *New Zealand Listener*, August 23, 1957, 30.

Jensen, Owen. "'Music in a Cold Climate': Review of New Zealand Composers. A Series of Twelve Radio Talks Compiled for the YC Programme NZBC." *New Zealand Listener*, November 1, 1968, 11.

Kitson, Charles H. *Studies in Fugue*. London: Clarendon Press, 1928.

—. *The Elements of Musical Composition*. London: Oxford University Press, 1936.

"Lavrentiy Beria." In *Wikipedia*, 2009, http://en.wikipedia.org/wiki/Lavrentiy_Beria.

Lilburn, Douglas. *A Search for a Language: Open Lecture 12 March 1969 at University of Otago*. Wellington: Alexander Turnbull Library Endowment Trust; New Zealand Composers Foundation, 1985.

MacLeod, Alexander. "Singing a Silent Song." *New Zealand Listener*, February 21, 1969, 5.

Mason, Bruce. "Mainly Music." *New Zealand Listener*, February 28, 1969, 15.

—. "Mainly Music." *New Zealand Listener*, May 2, 1969, 15.

McLeod, Jennifer. "Jenny McLeod," *SOUNZ: Centre for New Zealand Music*, http://sounz.org.nz/contributor/composer1071.

Norman, Philip. *Douglas Lilburn: His Life and Work*. Christchurch:

Canterbury University Press, 2006.

Ogilvie, Gordon. "Glover, Denis James Mathews 1912–1980." In *Dictionary of New Zealand Biography*. Wellington: Ministry of Culture and Heritage, 2007, http://www.dnzb.govt.nz.

Page, Frederick. "Alert at the Concert." *New Zealand Listener*, April 24, 1969, 3.

—. "Correspondence." *Music in New Zealand* 3, no. 9 (1933): 8.

—. *Frederick Page: A Musician's Journal, 1905–1983*. Edited and arranged by John Mansfield Thomson and Janet Paul. Dunedin: J. McIndoe, 1986.

—. "Some New Zealand Composers." *Landfall* 9, no. 1 (1955): 83–86.

—. "Some Twentieth-Century Pianoforte Music: No. 2, Sonata for Piano Opus 1. Alban Berg." *Music Ho* 2, no. 4 (1942): 3.

Platt, Peter. "Music and the Future Role of the QEII Arts Council." *Ascent* 1, no. 3 (1969): 42–45.

—. *Music History as a Living Study: An Inaugural Lecture Delivered Before the University of Otago on 20 September 1957*. Dunedin: University of Otago Press, 1959.

Pritchett, James, and Laura Kuhn. "Cage, John." In *Grove Music Online*. *Oxford Music Online*, 2009, http://www.oxfordmusiconline.com.

Prizer, William F. "Piccolomini, Niccolò." In *Grove Music Online*. *Oxford Music Online*, 2009, http://www.oxfordmusiconline.com.

Schoenberg, Arnold. *Style and Idea: Selected Writings of Arnold Schoenberg*, edited by Leonard Stein. London: Faber & Faber, 1975.

Thomson, John Mansfield. "Tremain, Ronald." In *Grove Music Online*. *Oxford Music Online*, 2009, http://www.oxfordmusiconline.com.

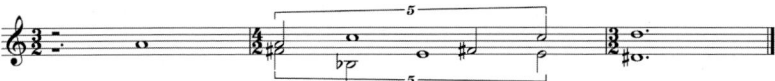

Figure 14-1. Transcription by author.

Figure 14-2. Transcription by author.

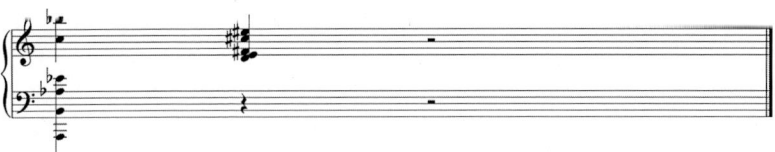

Figure 14-3. Transcription by author.

# EPILOGUE

# CHAPTER FIFTEEN

# NATIONAL IDENTITY?
# WHO WANTS TO KNOW AND WHY?

## GRAEME DOWNES

In a recent experience with government agencies (Prime Minister's Arts Forum in Christchurch, February 2008), the concept of national identity engaged from both the chair and the floor seemed to privilege that part of our collective psyche we might call a soul—at the expense of our collective criminal record. Indeed, it is precisely this charade of a comfortable national identity that the opening scene of the movie *Once Were Warriors* so graphically exploded, setting the film's confrontational agenda.[1]

Prescribed and comfortable notions of national identity can produce an uncritical cultural myopia, whilst history tells us that they can also produce arrogant, intolerant, and hawkish nations. National identities are—it seems to me—fractured, fluid, and evolving. One might even describe them as clan-ish, because values vary from one social group to the next. But if one group comes to dominate the others to too great an extent, we (as a race) have historically often had problems. Let's face it, an Aryan, national socialist view of German national identity wasn't particularly pleasant for other groups; likewise the description of Left-leaning sentiments as "un-American" in the period of McCarthyism. Both serve as perfect examples of how notions of national identity have historically been put to appalling uses. In my lifetime, competing notions of national identity caused a virtual civil war in this country over the Springbok tour in 1981.

It seems to me that defining national identity is nigh on impossible. Different segments within society may hold similar views, but contradictions are everywhere. One of our national characteristics, at least

---

[1] *Once Were Warriors,* Film, Lee Tamahori (Auckland: Communicado Productions, 1994).

on the basis of historical precedent, is pacifism. This looms large in the figure of Michael Joseph Savage, who opposed conscription in World War I and even in World War II, and finds its modern expression in our anti-nuclear legislation and our non-involvement in Iraq, meanwhile being involved in "peace-keeping" operations in East Timor. It cuts across political lines, such that the words "gone by lunchtime" with reference to the anti-nuke legislation can, and arguably did, lose an election. But our main sports team preludes some of its test matches with a confrontational war dance that climaxes with a throat-slitting gesture (quickly co-opted in trailers for the World Wrestling Federation, I might add). Our professional league team is called the "Warriors," whilst those who promote the game privilege footage of an on-field punch-up and a sideline-bound player, his face streaming with blood from what looks like a gouge. Pacifists? Yeah, right!

Our national identity may be a bag of contradictions, but what is worth fighting for is the freedom to contest it. At the Prime Minister's Arts Forum, my first comment from the floor was that, artistically, I'd spent my entire life at war with national identity, in particular with the narrow box of Pākehā masculinity that I was somehow expected to cram myself into. As a child in the sixties, I was fully aware that expectations of me were no higher than an appreciation of rugby, racing, and beer, and, when I got old enough, sheilas. The minister presiding over that particular session wasn't about to tolerate such sentiments and he immediately turned to someone else with something more uplifting to say.

It was a whirlwind day, the Prime Minister's Arts Forum in Christchurch. I'd like to begin by relating the structure of the debate. There were three simultaneous forums in each of the two sessions and delegates were invited to choose and attend the ones they felt most able to contribute to, or had some interest in. At the end, the entire group was brought together and the minutes of the sessions were read. I remember as the resolutions flew by from our session that some of the things discussed were present, some absent, and some additional elements had mysteriously crept in that I had no recollection of anyone raising. But, of course, a full two-thirds—those who were at the other forums—were none the wiser, nor did we have any way of assessing the veracity of the minutes of theirs. This made me deeply suspicious. I felt like I'd been given a free lunch to have words put in my mouth. Stakeholders consulted, we had signed ourselves in and therefore tacitly endorsed whatever was contained within the finished "document." It was certainly a lesson on how structure can so easily defeat public debate and the search for real substance. And how else, except via structure, can stadiums be built against public opinion, or the Resource Management Act contorted to make the Rangitata a braided river in name only?

I'm digressing into areas well off the subject at hand, I know, but knowledge is power, and structure is a way to manipulate knowledge to the satisfactory ends of the powerful. And when those in power want to know something, and there is backing for the Centre for Research on National Identity at the University of Otago, it is prudent to inquire the reason why they want that knowledge. To better enable corporations to sell things and governments to design propaganda to get elected? To know which buttons to push on the national psyche to goad us into going to wars or accepting limitations on our freedoms?

There were other things that happened in the Arts Forum that were downright perplexing, because they seemed the opposite of the consent manufactured at the hands of structure elsewhere. One of the MPs came up to me at the end and fervently said, "keep doing what you're doing," or some such. "Uh OK, what is it that I am doing exactly?" The then prime minister, and minister for the arts, Helen Clark, gave her closing address: "Arts and culture yada yada, more arts and culture yada yada." Then, completely out of context, she said, "you know, European domination of world affairs has historically been a relatively short period bordered by much larger periods of domination by China," then more "arts and culture yada yada." The disruption to the discourse was so marked that it seemed to me it had to be deliberate. Indeed, the *non-sequitur* was the communication.

A few weeks later, the Free Trade agreement with China was announced and the point of her digression elucidated. I felt betrayed that a democracy like ours could do a free trade deal with a regime that has the Cultural Revolution and Tiananmen Square on its record. Maybe my sense of betrayal has something to do with national identity, which of course is forged by history. Students spoke of Korean War veteran grandfathers who openly wept. Oh well, foe today, friend tomorrow; nothing is permanent. The British and the French have only been pally since the Crimean War after all and were driven into each other's arms more deeply by a unified Germany, and then a unified Eastern Europe under the Soviets, whereas before that they had spent centuries beating seven bells out of one another.

Where am I going with all this? Underscoring fluidity in national identity, just as there is fluidity in military alliances. And the need to speak openly about our society, because it is only through the discomfort it potentially brings that national identity doesn't become singular, rather than what I would regard as a more healthy, multi-faceted phenomenon.

It is important to realize that nothing about the human condition really changes—its basic and baser instincts—all that changes is the method of achieving those ends. Wars of conquest are, by and large, a thing of the past. We're a small and defenceless country, except for the vast distance an invading army would have to travel in order to conquer us. Pacifism? A luxury born of geography.[2]

In a year's reflection since the Free Trade deal was announced, I have softened somewhat. The truth is that we have always been dominated by someone since colonization, and have done their bidding in return. First it was Great Britain. My great, great uncle at the turn of last century sold his mining gear to buy a horse and a rifle to fight in the Boer War (you had to supply your own kit to serve Queen and empire). My great uncle died at El Alamein. Post-war, we were dominated by the US and paid our tribute via involvement in the Korean and Vietnam wars, nuclear ship visits and—in the first Lange administration—connecting into the global monetary system designed for their manipulation and benefit, as well as granting access for their multinational burger and coffee outlets that we now see everywhere. Now it seems that we might have to serve several masters, though, given that China practically owns the US, it is clear which one is in the ascendency and will increasingly need to be placated. Failure to render tribute to the new Rome, wherever it locates itself, has dire consequences for small, defenceless, vassal states like ours—just look at Zimbabwe.

Playing the video clip about the marketing teams selling the idea of invading New Zealand had two purposes for me: one, to show how advertizers use stereotypical notions of national identity to sell things—indeed they utterly rely on them—but the second video also reveals an underlying truth. We are, in any real terms, defenceless and always have been aside from the caveat of distance, which protected us in World War II from the Japanese, but no longer does in a globalized, monetarized world.

Is there no defence whatsoever? Yes there is, and it is the very thing that I outlined earlier: the right to contest national identity, the bedrock of which is free speech. We have a tradition forged by the likes of James K. Baxter, of being society's critic and conscience and we must, in the very best rugby parlance, "use it or lose it."

---

[2] "Ad challenge finds NZ ripe for an invasion," *Stuff,* July 7, 2008, http://www.stuff.co.nz/oddstuff/528685.

## "Rootless Cosmopolitan"

This song came about in part from the supervision of a Master's thesis that was focussing on notions of national identity in the work of the Finn brothers. In the process, we trawled through the work of three of New Zealand's most prominent artistic figures (Lilburn, Baxter, and McCahon) to find any commonalities between them in where they asserted or located "New Zealandness." What did they seize on? Māori world-view, God, and connectivity to the land seemed to be the consensus amongst the various commentators, particularly with regard to Baxter and McCahon. Could these be the pillars of national identity?

It would seem so, even from the first thirty seconds of Dave Dobbyn's "Welcome Home" video,[3] or Hayley Westenra singing "Hine e Hine."[4] Be wary of the title of her album *Pure,* however—impeccably tidy and unproblematic.

My song "Rootless Cosmopolitan" is in part a response to these cosy notions.[5] The first verse merely points out the obvious—that the early settlers were discomforted by being here and, clearly, as their actions would suggest, suffered from homesickness:

"Rootless Cosmopolitan"

Wind blown
To a strange shore
That we all thought
Needed improving
So we brought things
Like birds to sing
Something familiar
Some consolation

We're always blown back to
Back to square one
Back to where we came from
Never knew that I was one but I am
A rootless cosmopolitan

---

[3] Dave Dobbyn, "Welcome Home," *Youtube,*
http://www.youtube.com/ watch?v=HnZmCEdS7GU.
[4] Hayley Westenra, "Hine e Hine," *Youtube,*
http://www.youtube.com/ watch?v=JM1Eql4_fwo.
[5] Words and music by Graeme Downes. The Verlaines, "Rootless Cosmopolitan," *Corporate Moronic,* dunedinmusic.com and Yellow Eye Records, 2009.

On a dirt road
In a strange land
Full of rocks and
Fictional creatures
Where the sky's blue
And the whole thing
Looks like a billboard
For the breweries
(ch)

And I've stood, where he stood
At the base of God's mountain
And I can picture Jerusalem
But I can't picture me with them
I'd be fooling myself

As a small boy
At the museum
There was a bush scene
With brackish water
Like the man who
Stood near the water
Everything brackish
Scared me shitless
(ch)

The yellowing oaks of Mother England on the North Ground, the bird song of sparrows and, on the hills, magnificent crops of gorse in all directions, the consolation of familiar things. Do we still need them? Apparently so, at least in the nigh-on half century I've been alive, no-one has advocated pulling up the oak trees and planting natives in their stead, whilst the gorse—the magnificent yellow ruff round this fair city of my birth—seems, by its very persistence, to offend nobody. And what of that great tradition of a young New Zealander's big OE? Where do they typically go? London. More consolation? Why? The chorus answers.

The second verse alludes to Central Otago and the fact that most people will associate it with Speight's ads and *Lord of the Rings*. There's a big chunk of national identity right there: the love of booze and fairytales. More consolation?

The bridge references Maungatua, the great hill at the southwest end of the Taieri Plain, beloved subject of McCahon. I've stood there at the foot of it many times. My Uncle Andy ran a dairy farm at the base of it and as a child I was awed by its great size, how it towers and menaces. That and the stench of cow shit of course, which is for me the mountain's olfactive association. But if I were to mention connectivity to the land in a spiritual sense to Uncle Andy, I shudder to think how many expletives would be in his reply. Jerusalem refers to Baxter's commune on the Whanganui river (get over the h, Mr Laws), a more laudable effort to live out the triumvirate of God, Māori world-view, and connectivity to the land than Dobbyn's and Westenra's in my estimation, but one which I couldn't see myself emulating.

The final verse relates to my earliest memory of being confronted with Māori culture. It speaks for itself. At least I'm candid. I remember as a child how grateful I felt that my forefathers had somehow managed to subdue these warlike, scary people and that I had no fear of one accosting me out of what was left of the native bush around Dunedin. The Urewera terrorist raids of 2007 suggest others share this sense of gratitude in adulthood. Warriors are to be tolerated at Mount Smart stadium only—and in Dave Dobbyn and Hayley Westenra videos of course.

As a Pākehā New Zealander, I could never feel comfortable doing what Dave Dobbyn has done in tidily co-opting Māori culture into a sentimental rock video. I can't reconcile it with history, or with *Once Were Warriors*, or with a Māori woman at the place I worked in Auckland who, upon seeing I was reading *Bury my Heart at Wounded Knee*, asserted that that was the story of her people too. And for me this is the New Zealand condition, stuck between an indigenous culture that, whilst I am keenly interested in its renaissance and political evolution, I feel excluded from. It's like being Jewish: if your mother wasn't, you can't be. That, and feeling homesickness for a country that doesn't exist, is the untidy truth of the Pākehā reality as I see it.

In the absence of God in my life, not being Māori, and because spiritual connectivity to the land is for me a romantic fiction that economic pragmatism defies everywhere I look (clean and green? South Canterbury is, but at the expense of the Rangitata's braids), there is little space to move. In middle age I've come to the conscious realization that I create to contest, lest national identity drowns me. I cling aggressively to intellect and to being as faithful a witness as I can. Baxter's job hasn't been expunged with his passing after all. And I cling to the hardness of my European classical training, to harmony, counterpoint, and all that allows me to perform the deflating modulations and clattering mockery that underpins this track, in turn underscoring the tragic, ironic, even the untenable element of the New Zealand Pākehā condition as I see it. But hopefully with a little wry humour—being a Pākehā New Zealander may be untenable, but I'm stuck with it.

# References

"Ad challenge finds NZ ripe for an invasion," *Stuff,* July 7, 2008, http://www.stuff.co.nz/oddstuff/528685.

Dobbyn, Dave. "Welcome Home," *Youtube,* http://www.youtube.com/ watch?v=HnZmCEdS7GU.

*Once Were Warriors.* Film. Lee Tamahori. Auckland: Communicado Productions, 1994.

The Verlaines. *Corporate Moronic.* dunedinmusic.com and Yellow Eye Records, 2009.

Westenra, Hayley. "Hine e Hine," *Youtube,* http://www.youtube.com/ watch?v=JM1Eql4_fwo.

# CONTRIBUTORS

**Matthew Bannister** (matthew.bannister@wintec.ac.nz) is postgraduate theory supervisor at Waikato Institute of Technology (WINTEC), Hamilton, New Zealand.

**Dan Bendrups** (dan.bendrups@otago.ac.nz) is a Lecturer in the Department of Music, University of Otago, New Zealand. His research interests span Polynesian and Latin American music traditions, migrant musics and other issues relating to culture and performance in disaporic communities in Australasia. Research for this paper was supported by a University of Otago Research Grant and a Division of Humanities Research Grant, University of Otago.

**Sally Bodkin-Allen** (sally.bodkin-allen@sit.ac.nz) is the Academic Leader for the Bachelor of Contemporary Music and Audio Production at the Southern Institute of Technology in Invercargill, New Zealand. She completed her doctoral thesis at the University of Otago in the area of Early Childhood Music Education and is on the Board of METANZ (Music Education Trust Aotearoa New Zealand).

**Alison Booth** (alison.booth@aut.ac.nz) is a lecturer in Event Management in the School of Hospitality and Tourism at Auckland University of Technology, New Zealand. She writes on the performing arts and on the production of culture in local and global contexts.

**Shelley D. Brunt** (shelley.brunt@otago.ac.nz) is a Lecturer in Ethnomusicology and Popular Music at the Department of Music, University of Otago, New Zealand. Her research interests include Japanese popular music and music television, with a focus on issues of identity, community, and gender. Her recent projects consider the representation of communities in New Zealand music festivals.

**Graeme Downes** (graeme.downes@stonebow.otago.ac.nz) is a Senior Lecturer in the Department of Music, University of Otago, New Zealand, and composer in the band The Verlaines.

**Andy Gibson** (andy.gibson@aut.ac.nz) is a researcher in Sociolinguistics at the Institute of Culture, Discourse and Communication, Auckland University of Technology, New Zealand.

**Henry Johnson** (henry.johnson@otago.ac.nz) is Professor in the Department of Music, University of Otago, New Zealand. His teaching and research interests are in the field of ethnomusicology, particularly the musics of Japan, Indonesia and India. His recent publications include *The Koto* (Amsterdam: Hotei, 2004), *Asia in the Making of New Zealand* (Auckland University Press, 2006; co-edited with Brian Moloughney), *Performing Japan* (Folkestone: Global Oriental, 2008; co-edited with Jerry Jaffe), and *The Shamisen* (Amsterdam: Brill, 2010).

**Robin Maconie** (maconie@xtra.co.nz) is the author of *Other Planets: The Music of Karlheinz Stockhausen* (London: Scarecrow Press, 2005). His new book, *Musicologia: Musical Knowledge from Plato to Cage*, will be published by Scarecrow Press in 2010.

**Norman Meehan** (norman.meehan@nzsm.ac.nz) is a Senior Lecturer at the New Zealand School of Music in Wellington, New Zealand.

**Tony Mitchell** (tony.mitchell@uts.edu.au) is a Senior Lecturer in Cultural Studies at the University of Technology, Sydney, Australia.

**Marian Poole** (marian.p96@gmail.com) is currently researching for a Ph.D. with a working title of "The Influence of the Second Viennese School on New Zealand Art Music 1940–85: A Reception History" with supervision from John Drummond (Department of Music) and Vijay Devadas (Department of Media, Film and Communication) at the University of Otago, New Zealand.

**Aleisha Ward** (aleisha.ward@gmail.com) holds a B.Mus. (Jazz) from the University of Auckland and an M.A. (Jazz History and Research) from Rutgers University. She is currently working toward her Ph.D. (Music) at the University of Auckland, New Zealand. Her thesis is on the importation and development of jazz in New Zealand from the early 1920s.

**Kirsten Zemke** (k.zemke@auckland.ac.nz) is Senior Lecturer in Ethnomusicology in the Department of Anthropology at the University of Auckland, New Zealand.

# INDEX